While the Locust Slept

NATIVE ☥ VOICES

Native peoples telling their stories, writing their history

While the Locust Slept

Peter Razor

MINNESOTA HISTORICAL SOCIETY PRESS

Native Voices

Native people telling their
stories, writing their history

*To embody the principles set forth by
the series, all Native Voices books
are emblazoned with a bird glyph
adapted from the Jeffers Petroglyphs
site in southern Minnesota. The rock
art there represents one of the first
recorded voices of Native Americans
in the Upper Midwest. This symbol
stands as a reminder of the enduring
presence of Native Voices on the
American landscape.*

Publication of Natives Voices
is supported in part by a grant
from The St. Paul Companies.

www.mnhs.org/mhspress

Manufactured in the
United States of America

10 9 8 7 6 5 4 3 2 1

⊝ The paper used in this publication
meets the minimum requirements of
the American National Standard for
Information Sciences—Permanence
for Printed Library materials, ANSI
Z39.48-1984.

International Standard Book Number
0-87351-401-7 (cloth)

*Library of Congress
Cataloging-in-Publication Data*

Razor, J. Peter.
While the locust slept : a memoir /
J. Peter Razor.
    p. cm.—(Native Voices)
ISBN 0-87351-426-2 (cloth : alk. paper)

1. Razor, J. Peter.
2. Minnesota. State Public School.
3. Child abuse—Minnesota.
4. Abused children—Minnesota—
   Biography.
5. Ojibwa children—Abuse of—
   Minnesota.
6. Ojibwa Indians—Biography.
I. Title.
II. Series

HV6626.53.M6 R39 2001
362.76′092 B 21   00-69719
                                   CIP

For all the children in the cemetery at the Owatonna State School and for all those who survived but in silence.

From the Records of the State of Minnesota, County of Ramsey,
District Court, Juvenile Division, April 19, 1930,
hearing on abandoned children:

Miss Wittman: *This child, Peter, has been
    in a boarding home since October 1929.*
Judge: *What do you recommend?*
Miss Wittman: *Commitment to Owatonna.*
Judge: *The Court being advised in the premises,
    finds that the said Peter Razor is a dependent
    child and in need of guardianship, education,
    care, and control.*

While the Locust Slept

1

From high in the trees along the shady avenue, past Cottage Fifteen, a creature sang incessantly, and loudest on sweltering summer days. "Locust," the boys of c-15 whispered, when they heard the frantic solo. They were cicadas outside my window, preaching from the trees, but my child-self still hears their whirring and murmurs, locust, locust.

I walked through weeds on the playground to see grasshoppers of all sizes leap and fly. When they

settled, I watched them watching me. One, I learned,
the one the boys called locust, slept seventeen years
in darkness before soaring into the summer light.

. . .

It was overcast, almost dreary that day, the third Saturday of September 1944. I wore a soiled T-shirt and denims, and the slapping of my bare feet on the masonry floor echoed through the quiet halls of the Main Building. I rounded a bend and came to an abrupt stop. Miss Borsch stood talking to a middle-aged couple sitting on a hall bench. She smiled while pointing my way, but I sidled past them along the far wall looking straight ahead at the floor. I entered an office and placed papers on the desk but, when I turned to leave, Miss Borsch blocked the doorway.

"Peter, we've been looking for you," Miss Borsch said. "Miss Lewis said you would be running errands here. You must go to the cottage right now, get your things, and return here. Those folks in the hall have come to take you."

"Oh?"

"Yes. They live over a hundred miles away and need to return home in time for chores."

"What clothes should I take?" I asked.

"That's all taken care of. Just bring your personal things."

"I have no personal things," I replied and shrugged.

"Miss Lewis seems to think you have a pocket Bible and rosary," Miss Borsch said.

"Yeah, those," I said. "How much time do I get?"

"Can you take a bath, dress, and be back in an hour?" she asked. "Miss Lewis has clean clothes ready for you. The Schaulses will buy you dinner on the way."

"Schauls?" I murmured. "I'll try."

My thoughts danced between hope for a good life and dark omens as I showered and dressed. The rosary and pocket Bible in hand, I waited in the living room for Miss Lewis to sign me out of the cottage—for the last time. The matron said little, just drew a line through my name on the register, and my final departure from the cottage was of no more note than were I going out for chores.

Back at the Main Building, I was clean with combed hair, dark blue dress pants, and a light blue shirt. My Sunday suit and winter clothes were already in the car when I delivered the papers to the office. Miss Borsch stood beside me, and we faced the couple.

"John and Emma Schauls," she said, motioning toward them.

John stood, staring at me without smiling. Instinctively, I looked down, and we shook hands. His grasp was aggressive. I glanced up but his unblinking stare made me uneasy—like a strange chill had seeped into the room. He was only a bit taller than me but much larger, and his gray hair fringed a bald pate, prematurely for a man I was told was in his late thirties. Emma stood, forced an awkward smile, and laid her hand in mine, as she mumbled a greeting. She was close to forty and nearly cross-eyed so she wore thick glasses.

Miss Borsch's smile never faltered and she bantered non-stop about weather and farming.

"Peter has been with us all his life," Miss Borsch explained. "Now, he's ready to try farming."

I remained silent and stared at the floor.

My family fell apart shortly after I was born. The United Christian Charities of St. Paul was housing my parents and two older brothers at the time and helping my father search for work. He was from the Fond du Lac band of Minnesota Chippewas, named Ningoos at birth, and baptized Wilbur. He served with the expeditionary forces in France during the First World War and did not work much after marrying my mother in 1925.

My mother, Mary Razor, was quiet, given to depression. My father drank and was of little help nurturing the children. One of my brothers, Leonard, was hydrocephalic and retarded, and the other, Arnold, was still young. When the state social services ruled that my mother suffered from "confusion," they sent her along with Leonard to an asylum at St. Peter. Some of my relatives from Michigan came to take Arnold home with them, but they did not take me. They thought my head looked too large for my body and feared I would turn out like Leonard. So I stayed with my father. He was supposed to look after me while he continued searching for a job. Instead he went to Milwaukee. I was ten months old when he abandoned me.

The state placed me temporarily in the Christian Boarding Home for Children in St. Paul, where two months later a psychologist tested me and recorded: *Peter Razor is of Indian heritage. He is of average intelligence and underweight.* I was taken to Ramsey County court and declared a ward of the state, at which point I was ordered committed to the State Public School at Owatonna. My placement was delayed by a measles epidemic, but on April 30, 1930, I arrived in the State School nursery. I was seventeen months old.

The State Public School occupied hundreds of acres on the west side of Owatonna. Farm buildings, gardens, and croplands were west, and the campus east—next to the city. Most cottages, facilities, and the Main Building were on a central mound that created an impressive, almost medieval, skyline. The Main Building, a large т-shaped, castle-like structure, faced a street bordered by trimmed shrubs, imposing flower beds, and large, well-kept lawns. Visitors were greeted inside in ornate offices with a posh visitors' lounge and teams of smiling civil servants.

A private children's hospital had recovery and isolation wards and an operating room for general surgery, such as removing a child's tonsils or appendix. The hospital admitted all patients needing bed rest, including those with headaches or minor fevers. Cottages, numbered one to sixteen, separately housed boys and girls who transferred, as they grew, to cottages for older children.

In the cottages, away from public view, white-uniformed matrons reigned supreme. They lived full-time in apartments in the cottage and were called *house mothers* by the office. Assistants to the matrons wore colored uniforms specific to their positions and worked twenty-four hours on, then had twenty-four hours off. While on duty, they ate with the children and slept in small private rooms.

The school is closed now. Little remains but these buildings, and a cemetery at the southwest corner of the former campus. Nearly two hundred children who died of disease, accident, or *other causes* lie there. Those three years old or younger suffered a higher death rate than the older children—death from *general debility* or simply *wasted away*, the records say. Those without family were buried without ceremony. Children died on farm indenture and other placements, too. According to mortality statistics over one ten-year period, as many children died on placement as those on the school grounds.

State officials disagreed about how the school would affect children. About 1900, one officially recorded his concern: *I fear we have created a penal institution for innocent children.* But there were few advocates for children then, and their voices were lost in the din of politics. To pacify their critics, state social services declared they would keep a child no longer than three months. *It will be a way station for children, until we place them into loving homes*, they wrote.

For the good of the child, a family that had a child taken away lost all rights except visitation. If the child ran away from the institution and returned home, the family was obliged, under penalty of law, to return their son or daughter to the state.

Families selecting children would review office files and be guided by staff before meeting a child. Adoption and procedures for taking foster children required more than one visit, but I did not meet my farmer before he came to get me. I had no choice, was told nothing of how to act, nor what to expect. In an early discussion about my suitability for farm place-

ment, Miss Borsch said flatly, *Peter can take care of himself.*
Staff commented often how Dale and I ran away at age fourteen, were gone over a week, and that seemed to set the stage
to hand us over to farmers.

Most adoptive couples looked at race, intelligence, character, and their perception of physical perfection. Most farmers were interested in docility and durability. The bottom line
of my last physical, which John Schauls would have seen, read,
Peter Razor is a sturdy very athletic 15 year old. At the time I
was five feet six inches tall and weighed 130 pounds.

An institutional state ward for fifteen years, I would now
be a farm-indentured state ward. The state would not be responsible any more for my room, board, or clothing. Now they
would only pay for major medical expenses or burial costs.

Midwinter 1944 at the State Public School, Dr. Yager, child
psychologist at the school, posed a very strange question to
me, "Do you think you could call anyone Mother or Father?"

I mumbled, "I wouldn't know what to do in a family."

"It's hard to find a family for an Indian boy, and we have no
Indian families listed," Dr. Yager continued. "And you've been
here a long time."

"How long?" I asked, without really caring.

"Fifteen years," Dr. Yager replied.

For the first fourteen years of my life, I knew Dr. Yager only
as the one who sat blandly behind a desk pointing at tests with
assurances that no matter how I did on them, was all right. I
worked the tests at another table while he remained at his
desk. Dr. Yager loved climbing into the minds of children. It
was more than his job, it was his life. Every child had to be

somewhere in his text book or he became obsessed with exposing their peculiarity. He recorded that I was very quiet and, before the age of twelve, basically untestable. He might have suspected that cottage life was at least partially responsible for, what he wrote, my *sullen and withdrawn demeanor*, but probably knew little of my experiences with a few employees.

Weeks or a month after Dr. Yager's strange questions about family life, I was interviewed by Mr. Doleman, a social worker under Superintendent Vevle.

"You told Dr. Yager that you would not feel comfortable in a regular family," Mr. Doleman said.

"Well . . . I said maybe I didn't know what it meant to be in a family."

"Perhaps that was it," Mr. Doleman said. "Do you think you would like to work on a farm?"

"The work might be all right," I replied, then mumbled, "Heard it was dangerous. Being on a farm, I mean." Shifting uneasily on my chair, I glanced at documents on the wall, which said collectively that Mr. Doleman was very wise, indeed. I knew he stared at me, *into* me, and, uneasy, I looked around at the floor.

After a long silence, Mr. Doleman spoke, sounding like a preacher, "Everyone has to work for a living."

"A guy died on a farm last year, they said," I persisted. "The farmer beat him up or something." When stubborn, I pursed my mouth while staring at the floor near my shoes.

Mr. Doleman straightened in his chair. "You don't know that for sure," he said. He leaned back, slowly tapping his fingertips together in front of his face. "Unfortunate things might have happened in the past, but we watch things today." He seemed mildly irked.

Who watched Kruger and Beaty or Monson? I wanted to ask, but instead I mumbled, "Do I have to go to a farm?"

"Please understand . . . if you're not placed soon . . . well, you have to go somewhere." Mr. Doleman spoke softly, but I heard his threat.

"Why couldn't I go to relatives up north?" I asked. I squinted at the floor near my shoes. "If I can work for a farmer, I can work for relatives, can't I . . . or myself?"

"You're not old enough to be on your own," Mr. Doleman insisted. "Can't you see? If I remember correctly, you were quite run down and filthy when I picked you up in St. Paul. Miss Klein"—the c-16 assistant—"also mentioned how terrible you and Dale looked."

Shrugging, I whispered almost to myself, "You made me come back." Then louder, "The State School, I mean."

Mr. Doleman pushed away from his desk. "We'll talk again," he said with a sigh of disappointment. "You may return to Cottage Sixteen."

Called to the office in early July, I was ushered before Miss Borsch for the first time. She was young and vivacious, smiled nonstop, and her eyes were warm friendly things. Mr. Doleman had called up the big guns. Having no experience with girls or doting women, I'd be a pushover.

"Good morning, Peter. My, isn't the weather simply grand?" Miss Borsch breathed. Her right arm was elevated toward the window, her upturned palm sagged off the wrist with two fingers languidly extended. I watched her hand and reeled from her brilliant smile.

"How have you been?" Her charm was in full gallop.

"All right, I guess," I replied, trying to guess her next move.

"Did you enjoy the outing with Mr. and Mrs. Cory?" Miss Borsch asked.

"Corys? . . . Uh, yeah," I replied. More pieces to the puzzle suddenly fell into place.

"Have you thought about what comes after the State School?" she murmured softly.

"Some. I'd rather go on my own or to relatives."

"You became quite ill after your first, ah . . . trip last summer," Miss Borsch said, appearing concerned. "It's not in your file, but Mrs. Steele says your second trip was quite dangerous." She was referring to the two times I had run away from the school.

"I didn't think so."

"Anyway," she murmured, appearing sympathetic, "you can see why you can't be on your own. Just yet."

"Dunno," I mumbled, but I knew where it all headed. "Couldn't I go to high school in Owatonna?"

"I'd like to see you in a regular home, if possible," Miss Borsch persisted.

"Older boys go to high school from here," I insisted.

"Perhaps they want to do something else," she replied. "Go into the army, for instance."

"Can I do something else?" I groped. "Besides this farm thing, I mean. Somebody said indenture is slavery."

"It's no longer indenture," Miss Borsch corrected. "It's farm placement." Her smile faded, but she retained composure.

"And it's certainly not slavery! I really think you'd like a farm. We'd see that you got a good family, and somebody would visit you to see how things were going." Her smile could again melt steel.

"I don't know." Trapped, hating myself for letting her lead me on, I looked around at the floor. "If I went on a farm, would I go to high school?"

"Absolutely!" she said leaning across her desk toward me. "A farmer has to sign an agreement allowing you to attend school. It's your choice after age sixteen, but the family can't make you quit. And you are to be paid for summer work."

"Oh? Besides food and clothes?"

"That's right. We would leave the amount up to you and the family to decide."

"What do guys get working for farmers?" I asked.

"It depends on age and experience," Miss Borsch replied. "You might start at twenty-five dollars per month for summer work, but you'd work only for room and board while in school."

"That's a lot of money," I said. It was hard imagining money in amounts over one dollar. My grandmother on my father's side had sent me a one-dollar bill when I was twelve, and I had seldom possessed more than a quarter or fifteen cents at a time, since. Money bought tickets to movies in town or candy and circulated as part of a barter economy. Relatives sent money to children, and older boys, who seemed to always have money for cigarettes, worked in town or ran errands.

"You would get more as you grow older," Miss Borsch pressed. Beaming, she leaned more toward me, but still stared like most office workers.

I shrank back, my head tilted to one side. I wondered what would happen if I held out. I'd probably be sent to Red Wing, the state reformatory for boys.

"Yeah, all right," I said. My decision was not sincere and I sagged into the chair looking nervously around. Sighing my defeat, I mumbled, "When would I go?"

"A worker will check with the family."

"Somebody," I cleared my throat, "needs a worker?"

"It's not that you would go just for work," Miss Borsch replied, trying not to sound defensive. "But you'll be expected to help out. Anyway, the family lives near Rushford." We specifically discussed your Indian heritage and they say that's no problem."

Miss Borsch closed her notes. "It's settled then," she said with apparent satisfaction. "We'll call you when the time comes."

For a time it seemed Miss Borsch would make good on her promise to let me attend school. As August faded into September, I started ninth grade, riding with the other boys and girls to Owatonna High School, but the scorching wind of prejudice followed me there. One day the science teacher posed a question to the class. No one raised their hand, so for the first time I mustered the courage to raise mine. The teacher scanned past me a number of times. Finally he stopped and stared at me until I lowered my hand. I never tried to speak in that class again.

Despite the hatred of one teacher, those days were a heady time. I attended football games and pep rallies and, as the weeks passed, began to make friends. I felt better about my life and my future than ever before. Then, in late September,

Miss Borsch called me into her office to meet a man and woman who had come to take me away.

Interview with John Schauls from the records of the State School:

John: *Is anybody interested in Peter? Will*
    they stop to visit him or take him on trips
    or anything?
Social worker: *Peter has no visitors at the*
    school. The only one seeing him will be
    a social worker twice a year.
John: *Peter is just the boy I want....*

John thanked Miss Borsch and pointed at the outside door. "We's chores to do. Best be going." He started down the hall. Emma followed him and I followed her. We went through the large double doors and down the front steps of the Main Building to their two-tone green 1934 Ford sedan where I sat in the rear seat.

I said goodbye to no one except Miss Borsch, and there was less note of my departure from the school than from the cottage. We drove down the hill and past c-15. A pang of loss and helplessness struck me as I glanced back through the rear window. Then I sagged into the seat and stared out the side.

I was told nothing about a letter that came during the placement process, from relatives in northern Minnesota, nor of this reply: *Peter is well. Social Services is seeing to his welfare. It is important that he has no visitors, as that might disrupt his life with a new family.*

No one would know where I went.

2

Mr. Kruger, husband of Matron Kruger, was the first man to attack me. I was seven years old and in a deep sleep when a nightmare flashed—my arms were bound tightly and I was being torn from bed. I moaned, then froze when I recognized Mr. Kruger and went mute. Holding me by the left armpit, Mr. Kruger lugged me out of the dorm. My feet slopped the treads going downstairs and banged the doorframe as he carried me into his apartment. A newspaper hiding Mrs. Kruger's face lowered and I glimpsed her frozen smile. Mr. Kruger flipped me in the air and, when he caught me again, he gripped my left ankle in one hand, my left wrist with the other. Suddenly, I was flying in wide flying arcs, and the room became an insane kaleidoscope. I could only grunt as everything started to gray and I urinated. I must have sprayed Mrs. Kruger as I flew past, but I was unconscious by then.

I awoke, dizzy and cross-eyed, in the infirmary and was told I had been there two days. Hospital records describe treatment only, not cause, and I have no further memories of that day or the following weeks. Sleep and dark, after that, were frightening. My memory of the next three years is nothing more than flashes—like a lantern blinking in the night.

. . .

John sat erect in the front seat looking straight ahead. His shoulders were broad, his head unmoving except to speak—which was seldom. Even when he did speak, he seemed stiff, his comments awkward. He glanced around once, laughing, it seemed. "Sa weather look rainy, like cat'n dogs," he said, followed by a long silence. It was soon clear that he couldn't smile. He was stiff-jawed, and when he tried to smile he instead bared his teeth like a cornered animal.

I was glad when we stopped in a café where we each ate a hot beef sandwich. I sat on one side of the booth, John and Emma on the other. Emma talked little, mostly nodding and murmuring assent to what John said. Though I felt uneasy listening to them, how they talked and acted seemed normal.

18

Neither of the Schaulses asked questions of me. I understood that, too. Hospital staff were the only employees at the State School who asked me how I felt.

John seemed incapable of small talk. After minutes of silence, he said, as though suddenly inspired, "You to learn farming." When I glanced at his face, he stiffened with his head tilted back, aiming his eyes along his nose at me.

We first traveled the flatland of south-central Minnesota, then through forested hills with scattered farms. Valleys deepened and, as we traveled farther into the Mississippi River drainage, hills became bluffs. By late afternoon we descended a long, curvy hill into the Root River valley, then went through the village of Rushford. The road between Rushford and Houston twisted past farms and cropland along a wide river corridor. Short of halfway to Houston, John turned south onto a narrow gravel road, which meandered alongside a creek around high crowding bluffs. A mile from the highway, we crossed two small bridges within sight of each other, turning left into a driveway just across the second bridge.
"'S chore time," John said, stepping out of the car.

My new home was closest to the road and the other buildings stretched farther into the valley. The creek entered the farm under the second bridge, flowed along the driveway, and turned north to exit the farm under the bridge we first crossed, all within a few acres.

The tiny house sat on wood posts. It had a small kitchen, living room, and bedroom. The outside was white wood siding, the inside walls were covered with drab sheeting. Electricity had not reached the farms between Rushford and

Houston. Many had windmills and 32-volt wind-charged battery systems for electric lights. At the Schaulses, candles on the kitchen table flickered on windy days as if from someone breathing nearby. A water pail sat alongside a washbasin on a small stand near the door.

John pointed to a door in the living room. Motioning me to follow, he started up a narrow stairway that had two bends without landings—like sneaking between walls. Both of his elbows touched the walls as he climbed.

John motioned to an old bed pushed against a collection of household goods. After sleeping fifteen years in spotless bedrooms, I would now sleep in an unheated shamble. The gable ends were open vertical studs. John couldn't quite stand erect in the center of the attic below the apex of rafters, which disappeared behind the bed to the floor. There was space only for the bed and a fruit crate on which a candle sat.

"I go to barn, you to change, come quick," John said.

Anxiety burned as I watched him disappear down the stairs. I sighed and sank onto the bed. I wasn't worried about the farm, the house, or thoughts of work, but something gnawed at me. I tried to push that feeling aside as I thought of three weeks at Owatonna high.

John lost no time as I entered the barn, "You to pump water for the pigs," he said. He led me into the milk-house and pointed to a hand pump.

"I know about those," I began. "We were on this trip—"

"This is how it done," John interrupted, his face rigid. I watched while he carefully described how to pump water, but I could feel that gnawing again in the pit of my stomach.

My task was to carry twenty gallons of water around buildings and over a wood fence to the pigs. Chickens took one pail and two pails went to the house. My arm was numb before the pumping and carrying was done. At least the horses and cows watered themselves at the creek.

Supper was simple, but filling, after which we milked sixteen cows by hand.

It had been a long day since I awoke at c-8 that morning. Taking it all in drained me to near exhaustion. Instead of slowing the pace, John glared, turning brusque. What seemed like an eternity ended, finally, when we finished chores by nine o'clock.

John pointed to the washbasin, then the attic door.

"S'early in the mornin'. Best to wash your hands, then sleep," he said and nothing more.

I sat on the edge of the bed, my feet inches from the stairway. I blew the candle out, lay back, and was instantly asleep.

"S'time to gets in barn," the voice said. It was before daybreak, Sunday morning. For a moment, I didn't know where I was. I sat up.

"Bring lantern when you come." John set a lantern on a tread low in the stairwell.

Sitting, hunched sleepily on the edge of the bed, I stared down at the glow diffusing around the bend in the stairway. Slowly, I dressed, then creaked tiptoe downstairs, walked through the quiet house with the lantern, and pulled the outside door shut behind me. Emma remained in bed.

Swinging from my right hand, the lantern cast a swaying glow, flickering eerily through my legs onto the granary and the chicken coop.

John was milking beneath a lantern when I entered the barn. After hanging my lantern from a beam farther along the milking aisle, I faced John waiting for his instructions.

John pointed to the same cows I'd milked the night before. "Those be your cows," he snapped. His boy had taken too long dressing.

I sat and started milking on a three-leg stool. I took a deep yawn and looked up to see John staring wide-eyed at me. The long shadows hanging over his face made him look sinister. With my head against the cow's flank, I tried not to meet his eyes.

Most employees at the State School glanced at children, staring only at favorites or troublemakers. The first four terrors of my childhood—Miss Monson, the two Krugers, and Mr. Beaty—honed their loathing with hateful stares at certain children. Adults in Owatonna stared at State School youth at church or in movie lines. Their cold looks had always chilled me, but John's stare seemed different, even more troubling.

Emma didn't stare, she always looked from side glances toward whomever she spoke. It was a look of submission for John, but seething defensiveness to me. John had bought the horse, but she had to feed it and wash its clothes. It was clear already that she wanted no part of me, that I was John's to take care of.

After the morning milking, I was taken along with them to attend Mass in Rushford. The placement agreement stipulated my inclusion in family affairs. After Mass, I wandered outside until dinner, which included farm-pasteurized milk and homemade bread. After dinner, John pulled out his watch, "You to have Sunday afternoon off," he said. "Chores in four hours." Weekly leisure for me, however brief, was another requirement of the contract.

Climbing the high bluff north of the buildings, I perched on the steepest part overlooking the valley. The farm was over 300 acres, ten tillable in the valley, 100 acres of work land on the ridge, the balance in bluff-side woods. The valley was beautiful and serene through a thin afternoon haze.

With electricity and modern equipment, one man could work a 110-acre farm. At the Rushford farm, John needed a hired man to chase after cows hunkered in the ridges, search for lost calves in the woods, milk half the cows by hand, pump water, and perform other chores. When he couldn't afford a hired man or labor-saving equipment, a smiling benefactor—the State of Minnesota—answered his prayers.

I had completed eight grades plus kindergarten at the State School and three weeks at Owatonna High. Tomorrow, I would go to Houston High—maybe. Already, I was beginning to expect nothing until it happened.

It hadn't been quite three days, but it seemed an eternity. We finished milking and were in the house by seven Monday morning. I washed at the basin, went upstairs, and changed into school clothes. I would attend school without a bath since c-8.

"Youse to wash once a month in a tub in center of the kitchen floor," Emma had said.

"S'hard heating water on a wood fire," John had said.

Emma set a bowl of oatmeal and glass of milk on the table for me. "Be quiet so's you don't wake baby Mary after school," Emma warned. "She's at the Bensons'. She be home tonight."

"Okay," I said, trying not to seem confused. *A baby girl?* "Is there someone I have to see at Houston High?" I asked, standing, ready to leave for school. I raised a cautious glance into John's face.

"Be home fifteen minutes after you leaves bus," John said, his voice matter-of-fact, and that ended talk of school.

I stood and said, "See you tonight." There was no reply. I shut the door behind me, walked swiftly to the gravel road and, breathing easier, began the mile walk to the highway.

The bluffs broke as I rounded the last bend and the road thrust into the Root River valley on its last two hundred yards to the highway junction.

A call came from behind. I twisted without stopping to see a tall, yellow-topped boy hurrying to catch me.

"Hi, there," he repeated.

"Hi," I replied, looking up at him, and a smile warmed my face. Walking backward until the boy came abreast, we walked together toward the highway.

"I'm Ed . . . Hanson," the boy said, offering his hand.

"Pete . . . Razor," I said, eagerly shaking his hand. "I'm staying at—"

"Schaulses'," Ed interrupted, "I know. You just got there. How's it going, anyhow?"

"Can't say. They don't talk much except farm stuff. Got to get used to it all, I guess."

"We live on the table across the creek," Ed said.

"Farm?" I murmured.

"Yeah," Ed said, looking me over. "Just enough to get by. How old are you? I'm sixteen."

"Fifteen," I said.

Ed pointed at two boys arriving from a farm, which could be

seen on the highway not far from the junction. "Hey, the Busch boys," he said, pointing. "I'll introduce you in the Cracker Box."

"Cracker box?"

"Made out of plywood and junk," Ed said.

The bus appeared. It really was plywood and looked like a large cracker box, with windows and a small cracker box attached to the front.

"Sure rattles," I said. "Is it safe?"

"Guess so," Ed said. He pointed as the bus approached. "Lots of horses under the hood. Gets us to school every day."

Horsepower, I thought. "How many, four, maybe six or so?" I imagined teams of State School draft horses pulling the bus.

"Maybe 150. Dunno for sure," he said. "It's a Ford V-8 and Sam really gives it the gas."

The bus slowed, turned onto the gravel road, backed up, pointed toward Houston and opened its door.

Sam had a broad smile. I couldn't help myself and smiled at the ground. Sam greeted everyone as they entered, but held his arm out to stop me.

"Good morning. You must be the new boy I was told to look for," he said. "I'm Sam. I'll wait five minutes for those walking from the hills, ten minutes during bad weather."

Sam clearly meant business, but his talk wasn't threatening, and his smile never faded.

Most students hardly noticed me as they entered the bus that first day, and I ignored the few stares as Ed introduced me to the Busch brothers. Lyle, also a freshman, was a muscular boy, shorter than me with brown hair. Tom was in seventh grade, thin with dark brown hair, and looked to be growing taller than Lyle. They wore good clothes and sported healthy smiles.

"We're from an orphanage, too," Lyle said. "East of here. I'm fifteen, Tom's thirteen. We live with the Bensons."

"Hey, we're the same age," I said. "What kind of orphanage were you at?"

"Big church orphanage."

"Must be a lot of orphans around," I said.

"We had thirty to forty kids," Lyle said.

"Mine has about 250 now, but used to have 500 or so," I said, suddenly realizing the State School was a very large place.

"Wow!" Lyle said. "That's an army. How'd things go with so many kids?"

"With paddles and radiator brushes for starters," I said.

Ed whistled, then let the subject drop.

"Mrs. Benson is John's sister, isn't she?" he asked.

"Yeah," Lyle agreed. "She signed so John could get you. I guess his two sisters from Caledonia signed, too."

I looked out the window as the bus pulled up to a newer school building. *So that's how they got me.*

Ed walked with me into the school and pointed at a door. "That's the office," he said. "Just walk up to the counter like you own the place and you'll get faster service." We waved each other off as I entered the office, where I waited until the secretary approached the counter.

"Good morning, young man," the secretary said. "Haven't seen you before. Coming to school or just visiting?"

"Supposed to register for school," I mumbled, leaning on the counter.

She smiled, "I might guess the same. Name and grade?"

"Peter Razor, ninth grade . . . "

"Oh, darn, I hate when things are too easy," she said with a sly smile while reaching under the counter. "Looks like you're already registered."

I frowned, chewing my lower lip.

"Yes, sir! We're expecting you," she said. "Your transcript from the State School and Owatonna High arrived last week." She studied the papers. "Seems you're supposed to get better grades then you do. Well, you can fix that by studying harder."

I hoped Houston High didn't have any teachers that hated Indians.

"Anyway, here's your schedule," she continued. "You can still make it before the bell. Room 212, Mr. Johnson." She pushed a paper at me. "Good luck and welcome to Houston High."

I never found out if my labels from the State School—*mentally lazy* or *day dreamer*—made it to Houston, but my old millstone, *bright*, did. That made teachers expect more and gave prejudiced teachers something to disprove with ridicule and sarcasm.

Inside Room 212, I waited while Mr. Johnson talked with students. He didn't seem to notice me, until suddenly he had taken the paper from me.

"Let's see . . . Peter," Mr. Johnson said, scanning the schedule. "Come with me." He gave me a textbook and walked me to an empty desk. "Sit here." He tapped the shoulder of the boy at the desk ahead and introduced us. "Jorde. Peter, here, has your classes. Would you kindly take him in tow for a few days? If he became lost, he might starve to death in the corridors. I wouldn't mind, but others might." He turned to me with a half smile. "Jorde will show you around." He returned to his desk.

Jorde twisted to face me. "Hey, Pete. You good at algebra?"

"Not my best subject," I said.

"Darn! Thought I'd have help," Jorde said feigning a grimace, but it couldn't cover his smile. He pointed behind me, "That's Emmet, he lives on a farm." I shook hands with Emmet, then turned back to Jorde.

"Don't you? Live on a farm, I mean?"

"Nah. Wouldn't know which end to milk. Besides, I work in our garage."

The bell rang. "Come on, Meester Razeer," Jorde said, smirking. "Have to load our brains."

"Where to first?" I asked.

"Algebra. The more I learn, the dumber I get." Jorde smiled again. It was his trademark, a natural, permanent smile plastered there even when he felt bad about something.

Jorde pointed as we passed large double doors in the hall.

"Gym," he said. "Wednesday and Friday after lunch."

My first day in school went well, considering it was not entirely spent on studies. Jorde helped me in algebra, with Emmet observing, and I helped them in science.

Ed was a sophomore, and I seldom saw him during school hours, but we developed a habit of walking together from the bus to his driveway, then gossiping briefly before parting. Wednesday, my second week on the farm, we stopped, as usual, at Ed's driveway.

"Come to the 4-H meeting tonight," Ed said. "It's at our house. Mom told me to tell you."

"What's 4-H?" I asked, then glanced quickly at the bluff tops. "I mean, what do you do there?"

"It's a club where you learn about modern farm things and take a project each year to the fair," Ed explained. "It's fun."

"I'm just John's worker, he wouldn't go for that," I said.

"Heck, you wouldn't need a project," he said. "Just come have a good time."

"I'll see, but maybe not," I said.

John's car was gone when I arrived home. Emma tended little Mary as I entered the house, and it was the second time I'd seen the girl. Little Mary seemed always to be in the Schaulses' bedroom.

Emma didn't look up when I entered, just mumbled a greeting as I passed her on my way to the attic, and ignored me again on my way out to work.

Early chores were nearly done when I heard the car enter the driveway. Peering through the barn window, I watched John step from the car, testing the ground with each step as he aimed himself at the house. Wondering about his tardiness, I backed into the barn to finish chores.

Having observed how Mrs. Steele acted after drinking, which seemed harmless, I was not alarmed. Mrs. Steele, matron of C-16, was quiet, never abusive to me, appearing comical at times, especially upon emerging, unsteadily, from extended seclusion in her apartment.

John entered the barn to prepare milking equipment.

I called out a greeting.

John grunted.

I persisted, "Ed said his mother and them invited me to a 4-H meeting tonight at his house."

"We's work to do. It be late after chores," John said.

"Can I get off early?"

"You here to works. You in school all day, don't work to pay you keep."

"Six hours a day's not enough for my keep?" I questioned. "And all day Saturday?" My stomach ached.

"Not your age. Dat school's no good for you! If you quit school and works on farm, den you earns keep," John said, his voice growing loud, raspy.

"Okay, I won't go," I said, starting past him. "I'll get the cows in."

John stepped in my path and put his face close to mine. "No man's walks away when I talks to him."

I jerked my arms defensively up and quickly stepped away from John—a flinch honed at the State School. He stepped forward.

"I tell you everything. You so stupid, you still do nothing right," John yelled so loud Emma could have heard him in the house. "You don't to needs high school. I've five grades myself; I's highborn German, da best!" His face was rigid and his right arm waved close to me. I didn't move. My submissive pose seemed to placate John and he waved me through the door. "Now gets cows in."

That incident began my understanding of what angered John most—my desire to have friends, to attend school, anything that allowed me to escape him for a time, anything other than working for him.

Still shaken by John's diatribe, I was inattentive during milking. A cow, suddenly though gently, lifted her leg and stood on it inside my pail. Little milk was spilled as I worked her leg out, but greenish streaks of manure swirled in the brimming pail.

"Should I give it to the pigs?" I asked.

Saying nothing, John put an extra filter in the strainer and poured the milk in the can. It struck me as wrong, but unwilling to trigger another violent outburst, I said nothing. Days later, the milk hauler returned the can of milk. Instead of giving one pail of milk to the pigs, John had to give a full can.

Two more weeks passed. John was tolerably quiet, but seemed to be smoldering inside.

I walked with Ed from the school bus. "Think you could go to a 4-H meeting tonight?" Ed asked. "Mrs. Benson is a leader and makes the Busches go. Ma told me to ask you. She says you need to get out, and I think you should come."

"I'll try, but don't expect me," I said.

"Hell, if you can, come to my house and go with us. It's at the Martens'." Ed went up his driveway and I continued home.

The sedating babble of the creek soon lured me to sit and listen. A squirrel scampered up a nearby oak. When the squirrel disappeared on the hidden side of the trunk, I tossed a stick and the squirrel flicked off.

Suddenly realizing I had lingered, I hurried on to the farm.

Turning into the driveway, I stiffened with fear. John stood near the house staring at me with his head cocked. I moved to step around John on my way to the house, but John's arm shot out stopping me.

"Yer late!"

His eyes burned from a stony face.

I tried to move around his arm toward the house. "I have

to change clothes for chores." He grabbed me by the shoulders, spun me violently to face him, then pulled me into his chest in a tight bear hug.

I grunted as John squeezed me nearly breathless. I tried to scream, but John squeezed harder.

"When I talks," John screamed. "Don't to ever turn your backs on me. Bastard!"

I managed to bring one arm over John's arm to shield my face. For a frightening moment, he squeezed even harder as though to crush me. Then the world spun as John threw me like a sack of feed. Landing on hands and knees, I scrunched on my belly. The mauling more terrorized than hurt me, and, though able to move, I didn't, at first. Abusive staff at the State School seemed satisfied if I appeared weak or injured after their attacks. Watching from side vision I waited until John's shoes backed off.

Scraped on hands and knees, I stood and exaggerated a limp as I shuffled to the house. At the door of the house, I was forced to stop, but did not look back.

"You to come right home!" John yelled.

In spite of reassurances from smiling social workers, I now knew the truth of farm placement. Social workers, apparently, felt it unnecessary to tell farmers how to treat orphans, or to tell orphans how to live with guardians.

Emma looked up from near the stove as I entered. "Your pants is torn!" she hissed off the side of her mouth. "And you're mighty dirty for sittin', doin' nothin' in school all day. Not enough I cooks for you and wash your clothes, I have to mend after your foolishness, too."

"John did that," I said, pointing to a hole in my pant knee.

"If'n you'd work harder and not be traipsin' off to school, he wouldn't do that," she said, turning her back to me.

My life seemed darker than it had since the night Mr. Kruger tore me from my bed and I had first learned the meaning of terror.

3

Social worker: *John and Emma Schauls are a plain farmer and wife, share-renter family. Fifth grade education for Mr., third grade for Mrs. No interests outside their farm.*

Dr. Yager: *Tested while in grade eight, Peter comprehended most subjects through grade twelve. He communicates intelligently, scores very high in science, art and mechanical intricacies, average in math. He is creative in*

areas that are difficult to assess. He has the
potential to achieve whatever he chooses of
education. Recommendation: No farm place-
ment for this boy. It will end in failure and be
just another unfortunate experience for him.
His long term at the school has restricted his
social and emotional development and,
though bright, he would be at greater risk
among the general population than other
boys his age.

Social worker: *Peter is very bright; he can take*
care of himself.

Mr. Vevle [superintendent]: *I agree. In spite of*
Dr. Yager's objections, this boy is cleared for
farm placement.

 . . .

Despite the placement contract, John was determined to force me out of school. In January, when I still had not agreed to quit, he began shouting about school, flailing arms near me, railing loudly. He always began with some fault he perceived in me, some flaw he could not understand or abide. These rants would continue until he reached what was really eating at him.

"Youse waste time in school," he would shout, "while I works to puts food on table!"

Consequently, when I made the first honor roll, I didn't make a big deal of it. John said nothing about my grades, but showed his displeasure by keeping me home more than needed for winter work. After that I seldom finished a full week of school, often only three days—*Ees flunk and das school trow him out.* It went on all winter.

By February, when he had still failed to bully me into quitting school, John suddenly became almost pleasant.

"You quit school, I pays wages," John said. "If you stays in school . . . I don't know."

I worried what the state would say or do. Would I be on my own? Where would I go? John never gave me money for school or pocket change, so I doubted his honesty, but I felt helpless to do other than what he said.

"So I would just stay home now?" I asked.

"Writes letter to state," John said. He motioned to Emma who held pencil and paper, which she then put before me on the table.

"Tell them you tired of school; want to work for wages. Best goes to school until we gets answer."

John seemed pleased after Emma mailed my letter off the next day. The letter, which remained in my file, stated simply that I could not go to school after February. Work and school continued as we waited for a reply; John to have the state bless my letter, I hoped to have a social worker read between the lines and do something.

The Schaulses had a wood phone with a crank-ringer on the side. The six or eight families on the same line were each identified with a series of short and long rings, like Morse code. When the phone rang, Emma stopped what she was doing, lowered her head, and waited for the second series to confirm who was being called.

Mrs. Benson seemed to know that she would have to call

Emma if John were to let me attend a 4-H meeting or go anyplace for recreation.

"Rose called," Emma said during supper Wednesday. "They's a 4-H meeting at Hansons' Thursday. She thinks you should let Peter go."

"Be all rights," John said. "After chores is done."

I was astonished and ecstatic. After chores, I set out for the Hansons' house. A light dusting of snow made walking easy without a flashlight. Calm, so elusive at the Schaulses, now surrounded me as I walked between a gurgling creek and the dark sheltering bluffs. I stopped at the Hansons' driveway, where Ed and I always paused before parting, and looked at the bend beyond which the house was hidden. I took a deep breath and headed briskly up the driveway.

Mrs. Hanson pushed the door open. "Come in. Come on in," she said in boisterous, singsong voice. Passing her, I looked around at my laughing schoolmates and their parents, but I hesitated before stepping farther in. Mrs. Hanson leaned toward me. I sidled half a pace away from her—a reflex. She smiled and leaned toward my ear. "Ed's in the kitchen," she whispered, then pointed. "There he is."

Ed entered the large living room with a platter and stopped near me. "You missed the meeting part," he said. Then, with a mischievous grin, "Coffee?" I frowned.

"Don't make fun of guests, Edwin. Let him pick what he wants." I took a soda and sandwich. An older boy played the piano while almost everyone sang, *There's a blue moon over my shoulder.* . . . I moved my mouth but didn't sing.

That night, in my attic den, I stared at the candle through the breathing hole of my thick covers, then at the water glass nearby. Solid ice. The play of light and shadow flickered eerily on rafters and roof boards glistening with hoarfrost. I held my hands over the candle until they were almost hot then rubbed my feet with them under the covers. The candle was my only warmth, so I let it burn.

"Puts candle out," John said from low in the stairwell. I had almost fallen asleep and did not hear the door open. Blowing the candle out, I snuggled deep in the covers to block the cold.

When the snow melted, we began fieldwork. I shivered on the John Deere steel-wheel tractor in cold weather; John drove the tractor in warm weather while I walked behind a four-horse team disking and dragging. It wasn't just the cold. I was always hungry, more so than a normal teenager. Becoming lean, I moved slowly, without energy, which seemed to anger John even more. Restricted to one serving of food, I supplemented my diet with soybean meal and field corn. If I wanted more, Emma would always complain—*Ya eats enough for two grown men.* John gave his horses more feed during fieldwork, but refused to do the same for his working boy.

I hoarded any money John gave me and bought candy and nuts at noon hour in Houston; chocolate covered peanuts were my favorite. Munching from a bag on my lap, one day in history class, I didn't hear the young teacher approach from the rear of the classroom. My peanuts were out of sight, but the smell gave me away.

"All right, mister," she said, holding out her hand, "Let's have it." Though she was pleasant, I was angry with myself for losing food. I sheepishly handed her the full bag, and watched as she put it in her desk.

John let me go back to school on days he didn't need me. I missed a total of one month of school in the ninth grade, did no studying at home after January, but somehow passed with a C average. Emmet also missed school for work, but he wasn't in school Monday, the last week of classes. I was surprised, because most parents didn't keep their kids out of school at the end of the year. I asked Jorde if Emmet was sick.

"You didn't hear?" he asked. "Emmet drowned Saturday in the Root River, west of town . . . a whirlpool or something."

I twisted instinctively to look at the empty seat behind me. I was in shock. "When's the funeral?"

"Tomorrow," Jorde said. "The class is going." He thumbed through his text, trying to seem unaffected.

"I don't like funerals," I said. "But it would be proper to go. I would if—".

"I know," Jorde said, gently cutting me off.

But Jorde only knew half the story. Though I told him some about my life with the Schaulses, I never talked about the State School. I never told him about the children who died there, nor my constant fear that I might join them. News of Emmet's death brought it all rushing back.

Silver-haired and immaculately attired in a white uniform, Miss Monson lived for her work at c-15. She was absent only once in five years, that I remember, but her diligence wasn't for love of the boys. Miss Monson's passion was punishment. Her assistant, Mrs. Burt, didn't seem mean by nature, but she too had an uncontrollable temper. She assisted Miss Monson at punishment sessions, and, when a boy angered her, might assail them with a broom or radiator brush—whatever was handy.

The one bright spot at c-15 was assistant Miss Crusely, who worked the shift opposite Mrs. Burt. Miss Crusely never raised her voice or threatened children. She had little time to share with individuals, but every conversation with her was precious. I eagerly waited for her to arrive and dreaded her departure when she could no longer protect me from Miss Monson.

After each beating, I was gripped by a secret fear that one day Miss Monson would cripple or kill me, especially after my first funeral—for a boy at the school named Robert. Miss Crusely had us dress in Sunday suits and led us up the hill to the school building. We entered the auditorium amid a solemn hush. Miss Iodem, the principal, sat stiffly, eyes downcast, playing a sad hymn on the piano. In single file, we followed Miss Crusely down the center aisle, past the open casket, below the stage near the piano. Some children looked at their shoes or at the ceiling as they passed by, as though they didn't understand.

I didn't want to look but had to. It didn't seem real. We were the same age, and he looked so alive, his cheeks pinked with rouge. For a moment I stared intently. Would he crack a smile, call the joke? I knew he wouldn't. In that moment, I realized: by accident or neglect, illness or a sudden attack, I could be lying there myself with others passing by.

The sermon became a monotone. I glanced from time to time at Robert, saw again his rouged and puffy face. Afterward, we all walked to the little cemetery at the southwest corner of the campus where the service concluded. My fear deepened as I watched the casket lower into the ground.

I worked long, tiring days at the Rushford farm that summer. From well before sunup until well after sundown, regardless of the weather or how I felt, I worked each day, growing steadily stronger. Even John couldn't complain, but he never followed through on my promised wages or new clothes, so one day I asked him about them.

"You earns keep. I pays twenty-five dollars a month," John answered, visibly irritated. "I sees about clothes." I wore nothing but baggy, secondhand clothes meant for men twice my size.

On one Saturday in early June, the Schaulses took me to an ice-cream social at the Bensons'. John's older sister Rose insisted he bring me, and it was one of two times I accompanied the Schaulses anyplace other than to church. John's older brother was at the ice cream social, too. He was single, gray, bald like John, though heavier with a personality more like John's sister. Rose had a bright smile and, judging by the way the Busch brothers behaved, she must have treated them well. But I could not forgive her for co-signing my placement paper—giving me or any boy to her brother John. The social was pleasant, but I always felt out of place in crowds, so I stayed close to Lyle and Ed until I returned to the farm.

The Schaulses never hosted social events. John blew off steam by going to town and drinking, often returning home when I was half done with chores. The stronger I became and the better I took care of the farm work, the longer he lingered in town. As the summer wore on his tirades worsened. No matter how a horse got into the corn or how the cows lost themselves in the woods, it was my fault. If I ever dared to contradict him he would point upward and shout: *I's high-born German! Luxembourg! Da best!*

One hot, sultry Sunday afternoon, late June, the phone rang after church. Emma paused while staring at the floor as the rings repeated.

"Yes, Peter's here," she said.

I was excited, but dared not show it.

Emma spoke aside to John. "That was the Hanson boy. Him and Lyle want Peter to walk the creek with them."

Staring out the window, John spoke without turning, "Chores to begin at four. You be home then."

I moved cautiously out of the house, lest John rescind his approval, then hurried the half-mile to the Hansons'. Mrs. Hanson ushered me inside where Ed was already talking with Lyle. They both waved a greeting to me.

"How is Emma?" Mrs. Hanson asked, handing me a slice of pie.

"All right, I guess," I said, eating slowly so as not to not appear too hungry.

"I'd say youse are haying on the ridge," Mrs. Hanson continued.

"Yup, the road going up's bad, though we been fixing on it," I said. "Saw a great big snake the other day. On the trail, I mean."

"Be careful, lots of rattlers hereabouts," Mrs. Hanson said. She handed me a glass of milk. "Shouldn't have to worry none by the creek."

Beginning below the Hansons' house, Ed and Lyle took me

along a trail used by trout fishermen. As we meandered with the creek toward the highway, the afternoon heat picked up.

"Want to cool off?" Ed asked. We sat at the edge of a large pool. It was two breaststrokes across and maybe chest deep.

"Yeah," I said. "Why not?"

"Because we'd freeze," Lyle said. "It's spring fed."

"You guys chicken?" Ed asked slipping out of his pants and shirt and wading in.

"Not me," I said as I stripped. "I should rinse off, anyway."

"You guys are crazy," Lyle said, but he followed us in anyway. After getting myself completely wet, including my hair, I rinsed my clothes and hung them, shorts and all, on a bush. Ed and Lyle kept their shorts on, while we lay together in a sunny spot. A car whined down the distant hill, but we chattered on. Before we knew it, the car was too close for me to grab my shorts, and I lay face down while my friends sat back chuckling.

"Say Ed, do you think the Mort girl is in that car?" he asked, laughing.

"Can't say," Ed said. "Could be the Ladies Aide from the ridge." He pretended to be horrified. "Mom'll find out and I won't hear the end of it. 'Dear me,' she'll say, 'talk is, you and them orphans was running stark nekkid around the creek.'"

"I'm only half naked," I said. "I'm face down, I mean."

The car slowed but didn't stop and was gone in no time. We were still laughing as we dressed. Ed turned to me and pointed south. "Getting on to chore time," he said. We waved Lyle off as though we were headed home from school, but in truth it was much harder to leave them that day.

4

It was a Saturday morning after breakfast. Other boys had been dismissed while my friend Allen and me, at ten years old, were kept in the assembly room with Miss Monson, Mrs. Burt, and Mr. Beaty, the gardener and groundskeeper.

"Over here, touch your toes, knees straight!" Mr. Beaty hissed. He flourished the paddle near his feet. "How many?" he asked.

"Five for Peter, three for Allen," Miss Monson said coldly. "Allen first."

The paddle sounded like a whip cracking. I flinched. Allen grunted, rocking from the blow, but his fingers never left his toes. Had he cried out or lifted his fingers, that swat wouldn't count.

"One," Miss Monson said. She appeared more content witnessing the punishment of children than watching their play. Allen wobbled on the second swat, his mouth gurgled and he vomited over his shoes and spattered mine. He did not move or cry out. "Two," said Miss Monson. Frowning at the mess and stench, Mr. Beaty stepped to the side and gave Allen, still drooling bile, the last swat. Allen reeled out of the room to the bathroom.

"Now Peter," Miss Monson said, and Mr. Beaty moved into position.

. . .

The days grew hotter. We did field work in good weather. During bad weather, I shoveled manure while John was in town. Midsummer, a mother cat dropped a litter. The kittens were cute and, it seemed, we'd soon get a handle on the rat problem. Then, one night just before chores, John handed me a squirming gunnysack.

"You to drown kittens," he said.

"Now?" I hedged. "I have to get the cows."

His voice raised, "It take only minute."

Taking the sack, I spun around and walked to the creek. Holding it momentarily over the water, listening to the pitiful squeaks, I contemplated my options. I could turn them loose in the woods or hide them. Only John would kill me if they came crawling back. I fixed my eyes between the bluff tops and the creek and held the sack under water until the bubbling stopped, then hurried to get the cows.

Weeks later, a new calf was in the cow yard. John had me help the calf with its first feeding and prepare a clean bed for it. The cow didn't clean out by evening and, after milking, John led me to the cow's haunches.

"S'needs to reaches inside and takes afterbirth out," he said while mixing Lysol in water. "You arm smaller. Go way in, pull everything out."

"Okay," I said, not knowing what to expect.

John pointed to my T-shirt. "Take off shirt. Emma not like blood on it."

I washed my arm to the shoulder and did as John said, wincing with closed eyes through it all. Later, John said I got the bad stuff out.

Chores and farm work continued through July, and the second cutting of hay had been completed by early August.

To keep the sows, some weighing more than the entire Schauls family, from rooting, John snapped rings in their snouts. In mid-August, while John snapped the rings, I held the sows against the wall inside the hog barn. One monstrous sow reared from the pain, bounced me over her back against the wall, then leaned on me. My chest was compressed and my left arm badly twisted against the rough oak boards. Squirming out, I bent over to catch my breath, and felt woozy when I saw blood oozing from gashes on my left wrist. Quickly, I clamped my right hand over the gash, but blood immediately seeped between my fingers.

John saw the blood and, as though nothing was wrong, he prepared to ring another sow.

"I's ready for this'n," he said, impatient.

Still gripping the injured wrist, I held my arms up to force John's attention to it.

"Shouldn't I put . . . put something on this?" I asked between gasps.

John shook his head no, so I leaned against the sow to steady her as John snapped the ring. By then mild shock had begun to set in. I sat down again. John stared at me for a few long seconds, at blood dripping through my fingers, then shook his head again.

"You goes to house, get rag," he said.

Emma was baking bread as I entered the house. "Yes?" she asked, looking sideways at me.

"John said I should get a rag to cover my wrist," I said.

"All right, if'n he says so. I'll be checking to make sure," Emma said. She avoided looking at me on her way to their bedroom. Returning shortly with old sheeting, she tore a strip off, handed it to me, and turned back to her work. She offered neither help nor antiseptic.

I walked to the barn wrapping my arm with one hand while holding the cloth with my teeth to tie a knot. The delay was but minutes. I returned to the barn, and we continued ringing sows. John never looked at my wrist, never asked if I was okay. The cloth darkened red, but the bleeding seemed to stop before we finished. The injury later became infected, but it cured itself over a period of weeks without medicine or even clean water. Even after the infection went down, my wrist and arm were sore for a long time.

After the sows' snouts healed, fences were again ripped apart.

By the time I was nine years old, I considered myself kin to no one, so when a letter addressed to *Grandson Peter* arrived at the State School with a dollar bill in it, I was puzzled, but very excited. I hid the letter in my locker, reading it time and again, even after someone stole the money. The letter began my dreams of northern Minnesota, of other relatives I guessed were there. Nothing was said by staff, even when I received more letters, another dollar bill.

One Saturday afternoon within weeks of the first letter, I was told to dress in school clothes, and go to the Main Building. There, a social worker led me into the visitors' lounge where an older woman, a young couple, and a boy sat.

"Your brother, Arnold," the social worker said, motioning to the boy. She swept her hand past the others. "Your grandmother, uncle, and aunt on your mother's side."

I was stunned.

"We thought you might want to see your brother," my aunt said. "He's older than you." I was so surprised that the remainder of the conversation is a blur in my memory. For about ten minutes they sat on the bench while I stood before them. They talked and I nodded. There was no touching other than initial and parting handshakes, no explanation for why I was left. Again, no counsel was offered by any staff, no effort was made to prepare me for meeting a brother and relatives for the first time.

These were the relatives who, thinking that I would become hydrocephalic like Leonard, had left me in St. Paul when I was a baby. They wrote to the school superintendent asking whether I was of sound mind or not. Grandmother Sharlow, on my father's side, sent me the money and, I learned later, had petitioned the state to take me into her home. She was denied.

When I was eleven, Don and I slept near each other in a four-bed dorm on the first floor near a bubbler, the mop closet, and Miss Monson's apartment. Don had arrived months or a year earlier, was familiar with the outside world, and seemed adept at getting along with staff.

During evening and Saturday leisure we played in the first floor hall on the masonry floor. The living room was off limits except Sundays and holidays or when visitors were present. Miss Monson might let us listen to a Saturday football game on her little table radio. We played jacks, pickup straws, cards, or anything quiet while listening to the game. Often I settled with a book into a corner.

November, that year, Don and I joked as we left our play in the hall and headed upstairs to the bathroom. As we passed Mrs. Burt, who stood near the stairway holding a broom, I laughed at something off-color Don said.

"Deceitful Injun!" Mrs. Burt screamed. She stepped up the stairway, swinging the broom before I could flinch. The broom broke as it knocked me against the wall, its bristle end flew up the stairs and scratched Don. The blow stung my waist, but didn't bruise. Don's arm bled lightly, though he was more surprised than hurt, and he held it up in silent protest. Grunting without looking at us, Mrs. Burt slowly gathered the pieces and stomped muttering down the hall.

I said nothing and we continued up the stairs, smirking from the safety of the bathroom.

Saturday, less than a month later, Mrs. Burt hovered, broom in hand, over Leo and me as we scrubbed the hall floors on hands and knees. I don't remember now what Leo said to me, some whispered threat or slur. I whispered back, too loud, that he was a fat slob. Before I could move on to the next part of the soapy floor, Mrs. Burt whacked me again with her broom, breaking it over my shoulder. As usual, Mrs. Burt stomped down the hall with the broken pieces, leaving me to tend my severely bruised shoulder.

Boys could be selected to shower anytime they wrinkled an assistant's nose, or vomited during a paddling. But after Saturday supper, it was three at a time in a single spray shower stall. *Saving hot water for the war effort*, staff had said.

Assistants sat on a chair outside the bathroom and checked boys, three at a time, into the bathroom. When three boys approached, Mrs. Burt might hold up her dime novel and, squinting one eye, speak as though quoting Proverbs, "Wait on the bench, only three in the shower."

The evening after the second broken broom, my shoulder was sore and bruised deep blue, almost black when Don and I strolled up with another boy to be checked off for showers. Mrs. Burt avoided looking at me and talked mostly to Don, then thrust a clean towel and night gown at each of us.

The door opened and three freshly scrubbed boys in night-gowns came out. We entered, set our clean nightgowns on one bench, undressed to shorts, and waited on another bench while three boys finished in the shower.

"Burt's never hit me like that," Don murmured. He fingered

my bruise. "Except that time. . . . Hey, that was a broom what broke, too, wasn't it?"

"How'd you guess?" I replied, deadpan.

Don's eyes sparkled with mischief. "Worst Burt did was slap me."

"Yeah, why did she slap a pet?" I asked with a wry smile.

"Can't remember. Something I said, I think," Don replied. "Besides, I ain't no pet. Anyway, it didn't hurt."

"Probably just a love tap," I said.

"Nope," Don smiled. "You gotta watch her hand. And when she swings, snap yer head sideways. If it works, yer hair flies all over and you're barely touched."

"If it don't work?" I asked.

Don grinned, "She makes you hold yer head still and gives you another one."

"Smart ass," I muttered.

"I'll wash yer back," Don offered as we showered. It was customary for boys to wash each other's backs, but Don seemed too eager this time.

Don washed around the bruise, then suddenly pressed hard. "Ow!" I yelled, jerking away, banging into the glass door. "You did that on purpose." I shoved Don against the other boy.

"Hey, I hardly touched you," Don snorted.

The door suddenly flew open. Mrs. Burt leaned in, her nose nearly touching mine as she struggled to wipe fog from her glasses. Working through surprise, I joined the others with their backs to the door.

"What'd we do now?" Don muttered over his shoulder.

"What on earth is going on?" Mrs. Burt snapped. "It's bath

time, not play time." It was decibels lower than her normal range, but scathing, nevertheless.

"We're just showering," Don complained.

"Someone bruised my shoulder ... bad," I said, trying hard not to snicker. "Lucky it wasn't my head. Ever kill anybody like that?" Mrs. Burt wiped her glasses, staring harder, it seemed, than necessary to scold.

"Hey! Can we shower without people watchin'?" Don asked pointedly. Mrs. Burt puffed in disgust, shut the shower door, and left.

The threshing season was my favorite time at the Rushford farm, even though it was hard work. Each farm that shared the traveling thresher furnished a man for the crew. Too young that first summer to go threshing alone, I did chores while John threshed or, on occasion, we both went. The crew dinner included everything that was missing at Schaulses —smiling farmers, friendly talk, and food piled high.

Everyone there noticed I was different.

You must be Indian, Peter, some would say.

Others would ask, *Do you come from Brownsville?*—a town with an Indian community thirty miles away on the Mississippi River.

What tribe are you? everyone wanted to know. Once a farmer even asked, *Do you talk Indian?* But I didn't mind. They didn't ask these questions to be mean. They were just curious about what they didn't know, and in return they taught me about threshing.

At the Bensons', I watched the grain levels in the wagon and helped Lyle in the granary. John brought a load of grain and forked bundles into the thresher while Nels Benson fed the thresher from two sides. Lyle and I worked below Nels on the grain output when John threw a heavier then usual forkful—showing off—releasing bowel pressure just audible above thresher noise. Lyle snickered in my ear, I remained stone-faced, but winced slightly at Lyle.

John stiffly repeated something he had picked up years before, "A fartin' horse will never tire; a fartin' man is the one to hire." He then threw another forkful, while Nels politely chuckled. No one knew John's darker side. Even I didn't know that while John and I threshed at the farm on the ridge, a social worker was paying a visit to the Schaulses' farm.

Interview with Emma Schauls from the records of the State School:

Social worker: *Is Peter about?*

Emma: *No, the men folks is threshin' over the hill.*

Social worker: *Tell me, how is Peter getting along.*

Emma: *Just fine. He was on the honor roll a lot in ninth grade and little Mary loves him and Peter loves to play with her.*

Social worker: *Wonderful. Is Peter involved in school sports?*

Emma: *Oh, yes, goes out for football and things.*

Social worker: *I'd like to see him myself. When will they be home?*

Emma: *Oh . . . near milking time.*

Social worker: *Tell me how to get there? I'll see Peter at work.*

Emma: *You couldn't; they has to keep working.*
Social worker: *I believe such crews take breaks.*
Emma: *John wouldn't like that. You should come
another time....*

The social worker left without seeing me, reporting that she
was impressed with Emma's sincerity; that social services had
made a successful placement. During the visit, neither Emma
nor the social worker, apparently, mentioned my letter about
quitting school. The state had, in fact, replied by sending a
letter addressed to me. The letter suggested that I stay in
school, and that a social worker would stop by to see me. I
never got the letter, but a copy remained in my file.

That summer, Emma gave birth to a son, John, Jr., at
home. I had to work even harder, but by August I had not
been given one dollar of wages. I picked a day when I was
sure John was sober and asked him why. According to John,
contrary to what Miss Borsch had said, I had to pay for my
own clothes, haircuts, school expenses, and bus fees. When
John finished his accounting, I owed him money, payable by
staying home more the following school year. I didn't believe
him, but disputing him was pointless—even dangerous. So I
kept quiet, but I was determined to get something for summer work.

"Is there at least enough money from my wages to buy a
used bike?" I asked. "It'd be easier to go to 4-H meetings and
places."

"I sees," John said. Two weeks later he brought an old-look-
ing bike with worn tires home. He never involved me in the
purchase of secondhand clothes or anything I needed.

"How much was it?" I asked, as I ran my fingers along the roughly-painted frame.

"Twenty-five dollars," John said.

The following Sunday, Ed looked over my bike. "Your tires are almost gone, and the bike's been painted a couple times," he said.

"Do I need new tires already?" I asked.

"Pretty soon," he said. "But they're cheap. "A new tire cost about the same as your bike."

"Twenty-five dollars for tires?"

"Hell, no," Ed said, laughing. "Dollar or so. You paid twenty-five dollars for that?" He whistled, then frowned, "A brand new bike don't cost twenty-five dollars."

I stared at the bluff tops, realizing John had cheated me, but I had no idea what to do about it. "That's what John said it cost," I mumbled. John got my clothes and the bike at La Crosse, Wisconsin, twenty-odd miles east of the farm, the only city in the area with charity programs.

My working full-time for John over summer seemed to soothe him. Still, I needed to get away from him, and I was determined to go to school.

During a Sunday dinner in late summer, Emma said, "School to start in two weeks." She glanced sideways at me.

"We not done with summer work," John said.

I mumbled, "I have to go, though."

"You not to start yet, maybe later if we gets work done."

"Then, I have to tell the school and get my class schedule."

"Emma call them," John insisted.

I was beginning to feel desperate, "Rose thought Lyle and I could study together this year," I said.

My stomach knotted and ached from the discussion. John did not reply.

"I'm going outside," I said after I finished eating and walked up the bluff to watch the deep valley settle into darkness.

5

At mealtime we would line up outside the dining room waiting for the door to be opened. The door itself was glass and flanked by two full-length windows. Some kids would crowd close peering in, while the rest of us chatted and waited.

During line-up for breakfast one morning, Don froze, mid-sentence, and pointed over my shoulder. I heard the sound of smashing glass and spun in time to see Max suspended midair, halfway through the right window. Tiny shards of glass seemed to be splashing over him. He landed on his belly, head and shoulders in the dining room, legs in the hall. His T-shirt turned crimson, and streams of blood spread from his arms. He twitched on the floor.

Miss Crusely ran to him first. She held Max's head in her lap and gently rubbed his cheeks. Miss Monson called the hospital. A man arrived with Miss Putter, and they carried him quickly away. Don and I swept up glass and mopped the blood from the floor before we were allowed to eat. I couldn't stomach much.

The staff never said anything more about Max. Some of the kids said they heard Max died; some said he was sent away. Some called it suicide; others said he was pushed. Some said Miss Monson was chasing him to give him his licks, and he jumped through the glass to escape. It was nearly Christmas, and I was not quite twelve.

. . .

September approached, and John was off to town more than ever. I knew he didn't like it but his sister and the threat of a visit from State Social Services forced him to let me begin school on time. Three days after agreeing to let me go to school, John missed early chores. Emma ate with me, after which I went out to the barn to begin milking. I had just finished my eighth cow, when John arrived home from town. I was milking one of his cows when he entered the barn. He stood over me, glaring down his nose.

"Why not to milk some of mine with yours?" he yelled.

I neither looked up nor acknowledged him. I hunched over my pail and milked faster, my forehead leaning near the cow's flanks.

"You stupid ass!" John's voice rasped louder. "You don't knows to do chores right. School's no good for you!" He settled to milking one of his cows. I stood to empty my pail, and he was suddenly there standing in my path, forcing me to brush a cow's tail going around him. I emptied my pail and again he stood in my path. I had to step across the gutter to pass him. I sat and began milking another cow.

"You fucking bastard! I's talks to you, no walks away!" he bellowed.

He grabbed my shoulders and pulled me off the stool. My empty pail clattered in the gutter and the cow shifted nervously. John pressed me against a barn support post, holding both of my wrists with one hand. Unable to defend myself, I pulled my head into my shoulders and tried to turn my head sideways to avoid the stench of his breath and the crazy fire in his eyes. Then, without saying anything further, he tossed me unhurt to the floor. He went back to milking his cow, and we finished chores without another word.

At c-15, during Christmas vacation, Allen and I had cleanup in a hot kitchen after supper. We dragged back to our beds, tired from work. Shortly after bedtime, I sat up, my mouth pasty with thirst.

"Gotta get a drink," I whispered to Don. Walking in the halls after bedtime was forbidden, but some could, some couldn't. The rules, it seemed, were used to punish certain boys more than others and some not at all.

"Take it easy," Don whispered. "Monson's on the warpath. Been a witch ever since Max dove through the glass door."

"I know," I whispered, looking at Don in the dimness. "Did he die?"

"Nobody knows."

I had never seen so much blood, but my throat was burning from terrible thirst, so I slid out of bed and stepped softly to the door. I peered into the hall where nightlights dimly lit the tomb-like hall. Tiptoeing to the fountain, I drank deeply while eyeing the sliver of light under Miss Monson's door. Sipping my fill, I stole back to bed, ready to sleep. I thought I had been quiet, but soon footsteps approached our dorm, hesitating at first, then in that harried gait we knew so well.

"Jiggers, Pete," Don rasped.

I lay on my back, knees tight to my chest, staring at the door. Miss Monson paused in the doorway, then without a word, she stepped to my bedside and struck me with something small and solid. I jerked and she hit me again before the weapon glinted in the glow from the hall. A hammer. Held as a carpenter would. It thumped against my chest forcing a grunt out, but I couldn't feel anything. I grabbed at the hammer and was almost jerked out of bed before it came loose. I doubled up, knees high to protect myself, but Miss Monson kept swinging. The hammer cracked against my right kneecap, strangely numbing my lower leg.

Miss Monson wheezed some garbled nonsense. Her voice echoed softly, weirdly in the dorm. She raised the hammer overhead. For a terrifying moment, I thought she would hit me in the head, but she turned suddenly and left muttering to herself. For a moment everything was quiet and black.

"You okay, Pete?" Don whispered, leaning across the bed aisle. "Where'd she hitcha?"

I faced Don, moving only my head. "Hurts all over," I murmured, but we were very quiet so Miss Monson couldn't hear. I dared not examine the bruises. Certain that Miss Monson would return to kill me, I cowered under my covers. Shivering from exhaustion and fear, I slept to shorten that terrible night.

There was no indication, when Mrs. Burt snapped the light on in the morning, that she knew what had happened the night before. I sat numbly on the edge of the bed while Leo and Don dressed. Don winced at my bruises.

"Your knee's got a hole in it," he said. "And what's that stuff coming out? It ain't blood exactly."

"Doesn't matter," I said bitterly. Pulling my denims on, I eased to standing. "Yeah, it's sore."

Don looked at my chest bruises. "God, she's crazy," he said. "Shouldn't we tell someone?"

"Who? Monson's the dictator," I muttered.

"Dunno. We better get to washing' or she'll bring a gun in here next."

"She has a gun?"

"Oh, I dunno," Don said. "Mom and Dad had one in their bedroom."

Leo slept across the dorm from Don and appeared unmoved by what had happened. He was usually decent in the dorm, though seldom joined Don and me in conversation. His attempts to bully me, and others about the campus, seemed spur-of-the-moment to impress others.

All that day I hunched over to favor rib bruises and walked with a noticeable limp, which Miss Monson and Mrs. Burt ignored. By the time Miss Crusely arrived on shift, my knee limbered enough for my lameness to be hidden among twenty-eight boys. Because of rough play or a fall, as well as the overzealous application of a radiator brush or broom, it was not uncommon to have one or two boys limping among so many. I managed to conceal my bruises, but my knee inflamed and walking became very painful.

To scrub floors, we rolled up our pant legs and worked on hands and knees. Miss Crusely noticed I was not only favoring my knee but was working slower than the other boys. She sent me to bathe and early to bed. Not long after I climbed into bed, Don and Leo entered the bedroom, followed by Miss Crusely.

"You have a fever, which by the looks of it, comes from your knee," Miss Crusely said. "Scrubbing probably infected it or made it worse. You should have said something yesterday."

"It was Miss Monson," Don said.

Miss Crusely turned to him. "You boys can tell Mrs. Burt when you're sick or hurt."

"Mrs. Burt?" he asked.

It was clear that Miss Crusely didn't understand, but I didn't know what to say. Don looked at Miss Crusely a moment. He stared out the window, then blurted, "Monson pounded him with a hammer! Look at his ribs."

Her face frozen in disbelief, Miss Crusely rolled the covers back to my waist and lifted my nightgown up, "Let's have a look." She whispered to herself while inspecting the bruises. Miss Crusely seemed to believe Don, but she was helpless, for fear of being fired, to say anything against Miss Monson.

However, in the morning, she sent me off to the hospital with a note written by Miss Monson.

I was the only patient in a six-bed ward. Miss Pearl and Miss Putter entered, followed by an Owatonna surgeon contracted by State Social Services. Dr. McEnaney was a round man in impeccably proper attire with a smoldering cigar he seemed to carry, more than smoke. He had just arrived on the main floor for morning rounds.

He set his cigar down and examined my knee. He exchanged subdued comments with Miss Putter and Miss Pearl, then Dr. McEnaney probed deep into my knee. Pain surged through my leg—like all my teeth aching at once—but, when he was finished, his jolliness made everything better. The empty ward was eerily quiet after the doctor and hospital staff left, and light streaming through the windows shifted hypnotically.

Miss Pearl returned with a packet. She washed my leg, put salve on my knee and wrapped it with a hot water bottle pack. She started for the door, then stopped facing me.

"It's infected into a carbuncle, but Doctor thinks it began with an injury. How'd it happen?"

I shrugged and closed my eyes. Miss Pearl left.

The fever was sapping and I slept through the day, waking for dinner, temps, and hot-water-bottle changes. As night approached walking became very painful, but I needed only to visit the chamber pot at room center. A boy with a severe headache arrived in the ward that evening.

Miss Putter and Dr. McEnaney on ward rounds the following morning, lanced my knee, seeming unhappy with my progress.

"This blistering about the knee," Dr. McEnaney clucked as he worked. "How hot was the water pack?"

"It itches," I said. Stiff with pain, I missed much of their talk while trying not to squirm as he again dug into my knee.

"Peter can't walk on zet leg," Miss Putter said after they finished lancing.

"I'm not surprised," Dr. McEnaney said. "The infection is quite deep." His smile and knowing look comforted me. "He looks poorly. Perhaps supplements and uv therapy. . . ."

Miss Pearl returned with dinner, complete with six pills, which I would have with every meal. Some were for the infection, some possibly food supplements. Sulfa was important then; penicillin had been developed, but the military used it all or perhaps, like painkillers, it hadn't yet come to state institutions.

After dinner, Miss Pearl rolled an ultraviolet lamp into the ward. "Off with your gown," she said, "I'll be right back." She dropped a washcloth on my bed.

At c-3, one spring, we boys, age six to ten, undressed to shorts in the basement and were given a towel as we filed out to the front lawn near the main building. We were told to lie on the towel and take our shorts off, and the matron walked around laying wash clothes or small hand towels on each of us.

"We'll sun your fronts a half hour, and your backsides a half hour," Mrs. Kruger said. I did not know whether we were sunned for vitamin D or to treat a different problem, but I was embarrassed lying naked on the main street not far from the girls' cottages.

But I was too feverish now to be embarrassed; I pulled my gown off and laid the cloth in place. Miss Pearl returned to fit small dark goggles over my eyes.

"When was your last bath, young man?"

"Last night," I said shivering. "It's cold in here."

"That's your fever," she said. I felt her remove the pack and wash my leg. Then everything went quiet. A fingertip touched a chest bruise, then one on my upper arm, finally a large one on my shoulder. "Thought it was dirt," she said. "We play rough, don't we?"

She smiled, but I shifted uneasily and didn't answer.

"Miss Monson's note doesn't say whether you slipped or were pushed."

I stayed silent.

"We'll do your front for half an hour each day. Every other day, we'll also do your backside."

My knee deteriorated the following days and soon smelled rotten, forcing me to turn my head aside during lancing to avoid the stench. Fever and leg pain made using the chamber pot an excruciating exercise.

"Mmm, bad business," Dr. McEnaney muttered one day. "Deep in the joint. . . . Certainly injury-based. Perhaps the medicine needs more time." After the headache boy returned to his cottage, I was alone until Mickey arrived on my fourth or fifth day. Miss Pearl helped him into a gown and collected his clothes before leaving.

Mickey slept most of that day and moaned softly in his sleep. He had fallen off the top of pipes supporting the jungle gym, and he had compound fractures of both bones in his left forearm. Climbing on the pipes of the jungle gym was forbidden, but some children, including me, did it, anyway.

On his second day, Mickey sat up in bed, looked around, then at me. "Know you from school. You're a grade behind me," he said. He was pale and appeared weak.

"Seen you in school, too," I said softly. "Wanta play cards when you're better?"

"Yeah, I guess," Mickey agreed, settling back down in his bed.

As he improved, Mickey played cards with me on my bed; we joked and played guessing games. Though still mildly feverish, it was wonderful to converse with another human being. Between meals and temps, the hospital ward was a lonely, desolate place. Staff were gentle, but their talk was restricted mostly to treatment.

Lancing stopped after the first week and the knee infection healed. *A secondary infection*, Dr. McEnaney called it, spread down my leg in the form of pus nodules—little white volcanoes a third of an inch across, which the doctor drained as they appeared. Strange doctors examined me one day, but nothing changed. Eighteen pills per day, ultraviolet after dinner, and my temperature was normal by the third week. Then the little pus nodules were gone and I began to think I would really get well.

After weeks of kind treatment by the staff, my flinch lessened, and, without realizing it, I began to relax when staff came near.

"I believe you're filling out, Peter," Miss Pearl said one day during the ultraviolet treatment. "And your bruises are gone too."

"Ribs are still sore," I said.

"That'll pass."

"Wish I could walk."

"Yes, it's been over three weeks, but you need your strength first."

"How much longer?"

"Doctor will have to tell you that," she said, "but pretty soon, I'd say."

Sunday afternoon, beginning my fourth week in bed, the hospital was expectedly quiet between Sunday dinner and temps. Soft conversation down the hall was evidence of other patients. I was thumbing the pages of a *National Geographic* as footsteps approached the ward, and I stopped, staring at the doorway. Surprises at the cottage were often dreadful, but at the hospital, they made me curious.

Miss Pearl entered with a deck of cards. Nodding toward Mickey, she sat beside me on the bed. "Mick's sleeping, I see," she said.

I edged away from her, but could move only inches on the narrow bed. "Guess so," I said.

"What're you reading?" Miss Pearl asked, leaning to scan the magazine.

"About South America and that." I was confused by Miss Pearl's behavior, but didn't sense anything to fear.

"Want to learn how to play solitaire?" she asked sliding the deck out and shuffling it.

"I know two kinds."

"Well, I can teach you six games, then you can pass the time better," she said. She showed me the games, watching me closely while talking about things no employee ever had. She discussed my schoolwork, her family. She asked me about my thoughts on a number of topics. Other staff began to linger, Miss Plum on night shift, too, chatting for half an hour at a time on weekends. They gave me *The Book of Knowledge*, a children's encyclopedia, Indian books, and novels. No staff, including teachers, had shown interest in my thoughts before.

One morning, a shot of pain went through my knee while I used the chamber pot. I fell, spilling a night's accumulation. Wrapped in one of my sheets, I was carried to the tub by two staff members while the floor was cleaned and freshened. After dinner, the same day, Miss Pearl returned after putting the ultraviolet lamp away. "We're moving you upstairs now," she said lightly.

"Because of the spill?"

"Not at all. We put patients there who are well on to recovery." She wrapped a heavy towel about my knee as she talked.

"I feel better," I said, "but my knee still hurts."

"Even so, Doctor Mac and Miss Putter think you should be walking soon," she said, smiling.

"Guess I can make it upstairs," I said.

"We thought of that," Miss Pearl said, seemingly preoccupied with her work. "Besides, you've been in bed just too long and your good leg is weak. A maintenance man has agreed to take you after he finishes repairs."

I stared out the window, suddenly very uncomfortable. *Beaty? Kruger?* "Maybe we shouldn't bother him. He's probably busy and all," I said. "I think I could make it upstairs on my own."

Miss Pearl smiled. "Miss Putter says you're to be carried, and that's that."

A large man filled the doorway. "Where's this kid who's too lazy to walk?" the man asked. He was a young stranger to me and wore bib overalls.

I avoided looking at the man.

"Over here, Dan," Miss Pearl said. "He's not heavy, but awkward to carry. I appreciate your taking the time for this."

"No trouble," Dan said, approaching, extending his arms toward me. I must have trembled as the man slid one arm under my upper legs, wrapped the other around my back, and lifted.

"What's his problem?" Dan said past my ear.

I panted and squirmed in anxiety.

"He's stiff as a board; acts like I'm going to kill him."

"Oh, Peter's all right," Miss Pearl said casually. "Hasn't been held much. Take him to the northwest ward." She patted my arm as Dan started through the door. "I'll be right behind you." She motioned toward Dan's neck. "You'll ride better if you put your arms around his neck and hold on."

Miss Pearl's eyebrows arched and I quickly circled Dan's neck with my arms as we moved slowly down the hall.

"How ya doing, kid," Dan said.

Peering anxiously over his elbow at the floor, I didn't respond. Looking backward as we went up the stairway frightened me. I was forced to look forward so our faces nearly touched. As we rounded the landing going up, the corners of our eyes met.

"Good thing you're light," Dan murmured. "How's the leg?"

"Good," I mustered the courage to say.

In the new ward, Dan set me gently on the bed.

"Thanks for taking me, Dan," I said.

"It's okay. Get better, huh," Dan said as he disappeared.

Teachers talked about the men we'd be when we grew up, about becoming fathers, soldiers, or inventors, but we never saw any of those people at our school. I couldn't picture them. I had nothing but fear and hatred for Beaty, and Dr. Yager and Mr. Doleman were always trying to intimidate me. I waved to Dan as he turned to leave. It was the first time I was thankful to a man for anything.

The new ward overlooked the orchard, a winter scene of trees, snow, and the c-16 playground in the distance. The north border of the playground was a row of pines and a railroad. Boys came and went over the next week. Some stayed one day, some two to three days. Steve, with a broken leg, was wheeled in late one afternoon by Miss Pearl. After he recovered enough, we amused ourselves by tossing rag balls and playing guessing games.

In spite of not walking, I was at peace. Miss Pearl and others brought more books and chatted with me when they had time. After the fourth week, all treatments stopped, so I was more alert. I watched everything going on outside my window. Winter birds, c-16 boys playing in the snow, trains chugging past. I looked for the engine to emerge snorting and wheezing clouds of smoke from under the bridge. Long after the echoes faded and the last wisp of smoke melted into the pines, I thought where those trains were going.

By the end of the fifth week, I cautiously stood while holding onto the bed, feeling only a dull ache.

"Hey Steve, can I use your crutches?" I asked, one night just before dinner.

"Hey, I don't know about that," Steve hedged. "Ever use crutches?"

"Nope. Give you my dessert," I promised.

"Whadaya mean? You'll lose yours too, if we get caught."

"Then I'll give you the first one I get," I insisted.

"You shouldn't anyhow, might hurt yourself worse," he said. "You know what happened when I was in the hall."

Steve stole to the girls ward a week earlier. Seen by staff, he fell off his crutches rushing back to the ward.

"Well, I'm not going in the hall. You gonna let me?"

Steve relented. He reached over the side of his bed and slid the crutches across the ward. He then lay back with his hands behind his head, smirking.

It felt strange balancing on crutches, like learning to walk again, and I was weak, lightheaded. I leaned forward, moved the crutches one step before my good leg weakened. I shoved the crutches away and dropped to my hands and good knee. I was relieved when instead of a sharp pain, the bad knee only ached—like a ringing funny bone. I sat on the floor until the knee would stop buzzing. Too late. Miss Pearl entered with Steve's dinner tray, set it on his bedside stand and gazed down at me on her way back into the hall. She brought my tray, set it on the bedside table and stood over me, hands on hips.

"I was going to use . . . use the chamber," I said, higher than my normal range.

"See if I have this right," Miss Pearl started, trying hard not to smile. "You normally use the chamber near your bed, now it's in the center of the room. And there's the matter of two crutches lying all over creation." She reached down to me. "I'd almost bet," she paused before she lifted. "That the pot has not been used." She talked into my ear as she set me on the bed. "You're not to use crutches until the doctor says so. If you needed help, you should have asked." Her words were clipped with irritation, but she smiled on her way out of the ward.

That afternoon, before going off duty, Miss Pearl returned.

"So, you want to walk, do you?" she said. "The doctor thinks you're ready."

She held me about the waist and helped me walk about my bed.

The next afternoon, I was ordered to sit in a chair for an hour before the exercise. After more days, I walked alone with Miss Pearl watching, then for the smiling doctor one morning. I soon could walk continuously around the ward, finding it less perilous to use the chamber pot.

The nurses continued to show me things, talk with me, and bring more books. Before long I was able to walk on my own. My disability had been the result of damaged cartilage, both from the hammer attack itself and the infection from scrubbing floors on the open wound. In the end, it was enough to put me in the hospital for over three months, but it was a veiled blessing. In those months, I conversed more hours with staff outside their duties than I had in all my previous years. When my knee became firm enough to support me for long periods, I returned to c-15.

After two weeks of school, John kept me home on the Rushford farm for a full week.

"We's to shock corn," he said. I went to school the following week, after which I immediately lost another week of school. "We's to get winter wood," he said. I missed another week in October; then many single days throughout the fall, at least one per week.

With no provision in the contract for wages during the school year, my missing weeks of school meant that John got his work done, paid no lunch or bus fees, and still didn't pay wages. Not that he would have paid me, but his bookkeeping was simplified and, if he played his cards right, I'd fail school. Fortunately for John, Social Services did not check his finances. Nor did they force him, as the placement contract stipulated, to put a fixed portion of my wages in a trust fund, which would have been returned to me at age eighteen.

My classes were not hard that fall, but missing so much school, as I had during ninth grade, I found it difficult to maintain passing grades. Most of my teachers were sympathetic—except my gym coach, Mr. Heiman. He wanted all boys dressed alike and always ridiculed my State School gym shorts and sleeveless T-shirt. Teachers at Houston couldn't touch the students—unlike at the State School, where even teachers slapped students and whacked them with paddles and rulers. Mr. Heiman had to be more careful. Once he tried to get me a beating and make it appear the luck of the draw.

Our class entered the gymnasium Wednesday and lined up for roll call.

"What're the mats for?" I whispered to Jorde, and pointed at four mats forming a square in the center of gym.

"Boxing," Jorde said, nodding at the door.

Talk was that Jorde was a good boxer. I was glad for him so long as I didn't have to box. I did not box at the State School, Owatonna High, nor during ninth grade at Houston High. Boxing at the State School was extracurricular or for the Golden Gloves. Hard work and a meager diet kept me leaner than most boys my weight.

Mr. Heiman entered holding two pair of boxing gloves by the ties. He pointed to the mats and said, "We're going to box today, one match at a time." He gazed down the line of boys as he sidled near Jorde. "Jorde's a good boxer, I'll have him start. The rest can take pointers." He handed Jorde a pair of gloves, and casually scanned the class before returning his gaze to me.

"You look about Jorde's weight. Step over to the scale with him."

"I can't box; don't like to neither," I said.

"Do you want a failure for the day?" Mr. Heiman snapped. His faced hardened.

"All right by me," I replied, hoping that would end the matter.

"You're not afraid, are you?" Mr. Heiman persisted, speaking loud enough so all could hear.

"That's not it—"

He started to laugh.

I breathed deeply and reached for the gloves, "All right, I'll do it."

I did not expect to be ridiculed into boxing in a high school gym class. Boxing was fighting; fighting meant anger, and I certainly didn't want to fight a friend.

Jorde's smile failed to hide a flicker of discomfort on his face. "We'll just spar, Pete," he said as our gloves were tied on. "What is it, anyhow, couple minutes?"

Jorde weighed in heavier than me, but within the allowable weight spread. We were both five-foot eight.

Mr. Heiman blew his whistle; we touched gloves and began to spar. I shuffled with firmly planted feet while Jorde danced. Our gloves slapped and I swung halfhearted until Jorde snapped my head, almost making me fall. The jab hurt, and friends were not supposed to hurt each other, even in sport. I suddenly wanted to put boxing behind me—Jorde would have to pay for the teacher's prejudice. Taking two deliberate steps forward—street fighting—ignoring Jorde, I waded through his guard and gave him two very hard blows to the head. I was still sore from the sow accident, and pain shot through my wrist. Jorde went flat on his back, stunned, then slowly propped on his elbows, blood streaming from his nose and mouth. If Jorde was surprised, I was even more so and Mr. Heiman, perhaps, the most. His plan had backfired.

The mats were removed and Mr. Heiman ordered basketball relays while he gave Jorde first-aid. In spite of Mr. Heiman being there, I knelt beside Jorde offering my hand.

Jorde's permanent smile showed through a grimace while he shook my hand and said nasally, "You sure got a swing. You should hit John like that."

6

One night when I was about three years old, staying in c-6, I awoke in the lap of the matron. She rocked me and caressed my back. I don't know why she might have taken me from my bed, whether I was sick or maybe having a nightmare. All I remember is that she held me there, comforting me, until I slept. It stands alone in my memories of childhood. It was the only time I was ever held, and, because of that, it remains one of the strangest and happiest moments of my early life.

. . .

In early November, John tied a butcher steer to a post in the cow yard. I sat on the fence to distance myself from the slaughter, but John held up the sledgehammer and pointed to the animal's forehead.

"Come, you to hit there," he said.

I didn't want to do it, but to avoid John's anger, I stepped down, slowly made my way to John, and took the sledge. Biting my lower lip, I lifted the sledge and closed my eyes. I hit the steer on the head with a thud. The steer bellowed and sagged to its knees, its head swaying. I dropped the sledge and stared at the beast.

"You to hit again. That not hard enough," John said. He picked up the sledge and thrust it at me.

"I'm not strong enough," I cried. The steer was twitching and kicking.

"Asshole," John said.

He took the sledge and hit the animal. I heard the sound of bones crushing. The steer kicked one last time and was dead. The meat was taken to Rushford and stored in a rented locker.

I attended school regularly through the rest of November and until Christmas vacation. Early December, John began to leave the farm after morning chores and didn't return until I had started evening chores. He was preparing to rent a small farm near Caledonia. He drank a lot at this time. I was used to his tirades when he drank, but now he openly berated Emma, too.

I had little idea what went on privately between the Schaulses'. Emma knew that John could run a small farm without me, and she was pressing, though I didn't know it then, to get rid of me. Whether John wanted the security of having his work done while he binged in town or he had to have someone to intimidate, he seemed intent on keeping me around. I knew we were going to Caledonia, but John would say nothing of a future school, and as far as Houston High was concerned, when I turned in my books, I was simply dropping out.

Days before Christmas, the landlord paid us a visit. He was a stout man, well-dressed, in his thirties with a business-like demeanor, but kind. On a Sunday, weeks earlier, he had stopped by the farm and taken me squirrel hunting on a ridge farm he also owned. He seemed to have taken a liking to me.

"Have a few things for the family," he told Emma. "Can't stay. Just wanted to wish you all a Merry Christmas." He handed a sack to Emma, then turned to me. "Merry Christmas to you, too, Peter. Here's a sweater for school and there's another gift for you in the sack."

Inside the sack were socks and a billfold, which would hold nothing for some time to come. "Thanks," I said.

We began moving over Christmas vacation to the Lange farm, two miles northwest of Caledonia on a county road serviced by the school bus. The farm had been the Lange family home until they bought a tavern in Caledonia where they lived above the bar. Emma sent Mary and John, Jr., to the Bensons while we moved. Though the distance was only fourteen miles, hauling farm equipment and household goods was hard, cold work. We had to milk and do regular chores through it all and, thankfully, John drank little during the move. We often had others, including his brother, helping.

On the last day, a truck arrived after morning chores. We

moved the cows to the Caledonia farm and milked them that night under electric lights in a different barn. We were completely moved by the first of the year.

Officially separated from Houston High during Christmas vacation, I looked forward to Caledonia High, but knew John had other plans. My move from Rushford to Caledonia became a loss, not only of friends, but of an important check on John's behavior. Rose Benson could no longer help me.

After my six weeks in the hospital, I feared that Miss Monson would attack me again, but I returned to a cottage with no more corporal punishment and no restrictions on walking in the halls after bedtime. Things seemed to improve. One evening that summer, the kids from all cottages were allowed to go to the gym and watch the older State School boys play basketball against the boys from the State School for the Deaf in Faribault. Another night, Miss Crusely organized a carnival in the c-15 basement giving us another evening of excitement, playing games of ring-toss and lobbing balls into cups, with popcorn balls as prizes. When summer arrived, there were picnics at Mineral Springs, just out of town, and bus rides to Clear Lake in Waseca, thirteen miles away. Swimming at the gravel pit and other trips into town were a chance to get near, but not yet talk to, girls our own age.

The only activity I shared with girls was school. Puberty was upon us, but the staff never explained anything about relationships with girls. They quoted Scriptures or other authority, then left us to figure things out for ourselves. They didn't even help us with the basics of conversation. The staff taught us to shake hands, say good morning and goodbye, but nothing of those rituals binding people to each other and society. But my dark years in c-15 were about to end.

After breakfast one morning in the assembly room, Mrs. Burt pointed to me and said, "You're going to c-16 this morning."

Mrs. Burt saw me out the back door of c-15 for the last time. "Give this to Mrs. Steele soon's you get there, or you'll miss dinner," she said, thrusting a paper at me. She said no more and did not offer her hand, which seemed perfectly normal after five years with her. She had only touched me with brooms and radiator brushes—and to hold my lips shut while she squeezed my cheeks to make sure the soap foamed. My personal possessions in one hand, State School clothes over the other arm, I walked away without looking back.

I was met at the door of c-16 by Matron Mrs. Steele and Mrs. Cory, an assistant. The matron was middle-aged or younger, and slightly overweight, with graying black hair.

"Peter Razor, is it?" Mrs. Steele said. She pulled a folder from under her arm and scanned it. "It seems you have a knee problem. How is it?" She glanced at my torn denims.

"Okay," I said.

"You're hard on pants, too," she said, then raised her voice. "Miss Monson thinks you trifle too much."

"What?"

Dale Cole appeared in my side vision.

"Well, keep your nose clean and you'll get along," she said. "Mrs. Cory will explain the rules." She aimed her thumb toward Mrs. Cory.

"There'll be no chores today," Mrs. Cory said, as Mrs.

Steele headed for her apartment. "You can get acquainted with the grounds until dinner. Come Monday you'll work in the gardens."

I frowned, thinking of Mr. Beaty.

Mrs. Cory faced Dale, "You know each other?"

"Yeah," we both responded.

"Good," she said, turning to Dale. "Show Peter around, but get him back in time for dinner. And don't leave the grounds just yet."

Miss Klein, on the other shift, was also decent to me. Still in her early thirties, she wore glasses and her brown hair had a neat perm. She was pleasantly uncomplicated, doing what the matron expected of her. A boy could argue with her, even talk her down, but she never veered from schedules. Little out of the ordinary happened my first months at c-16; working for Mr. Beaty in the gardens was tolerable and the dark discomfort of c-3 and c-15 seemed to fade.

The thirty-two boys in c-16 ranged in age from twelve through high school. It was confusing at first, sleeping near and working with older boys. Their talk was strange, even dull at times—about girls, work, errands in town, or athletics. Hierarchies seemed driven by hormones in one sense, age in another. But, with its variety of talents among scholars and athletes, c-16 became interesting. Some smoked, others had friends from the girls' cottages. There were no individual lessons in music or dance, of which I was aware, nor counseling on making friends with girls. Boys who danced or played instruments, and those understanding boy-girl relationships, brought their skills from real homes.

Mrs. Cory sent me to work occasionally for Mr. Distad, the

storeroom supervisor whose office was amid the clutter of incoming and outgoing supplies in the basement of the Main Building. *Peter is a good worker, converses intelligently . . . is a pleasure to have around*, Mr. Distad wrote. Polio had left him paralyzed and confined to a wheelchair. He was the first male employee to talk about things outside our work, and give work instructions in a thoughtful, kindly manner. Few employees disputed the first assessment of a child, but Mr. Distad was willing to frame his own opinions.

The Schaulses' move from Rushford to Caledonia afforded us certain comforts. We had hot and cold running water in the house and barn and an inside bathroom, and I had a warm bedroom. With electricity, I no longer needed candles, which had all but prohibited reading in bed, the only place I could. My bedroom was spacious with hardwood flooring, a chair, table, and a heat grate opening down to the living room. A small domestic refrigerator, the likes of which I had never seen, dominated the kitchen.

Chores became even easier when John bought a portable milker for two cows at a time. We were no sooner settled on the new farm, however, than John's ranting began. I kept hoping they would send me away.

We sat for supper on a cold day in January.

"We don't need Peter no more," Emma said. "They's electricity and a milker, and the fields is close to the buildings. He's been nothing but trouble since we took him."

"Maybe he iss dumb. He do chores and help with work," John said.

"That's what you says," Emma said. "Who has to wash and

mend his clothes? You give me barely enough money for food."

"Watch your mouth, woman. I puts food on the table and works the farm. I sees he earns keep."

I knew John would get his way. He always did. Excusing myself, I went to the barn to prepare for milking. No matter what they said, I wasn't too young or dumb to escape life with the Schaulses. I was, by now, too numb.

John could hide his violations of the contract in the matter of my wages, negligence, and outright abuse from overworked social workers who were more interested in checking off a visit to a client than in search for problems. By keeping me out of school against my wishes, however, John visibly stretched the placement contract to default. Four weeks had passed since Christmas vacation, and John still kept me home.

He couldn't ignore a letter from State Social Services in early February, however, which he and Emma discussed in the living room. Enough of their conversation drifted up through the heat grate for me to understand.

"They wonder if we're doing good on the new farm," Emma said. "What do we tell them?"

"Dat ever'tings good and Peter's good," John replied.

"They wonder how he's doing in school," Emma said. She sounded nervous.

"Maybe tink of something," John said.

"You tell them, I'm not saying he's in school when he hain't," Emma said. "When're you going to send him away, inahow?"

After hushed talk, John spoke louder, "Maybe we let him go school for now."

That Friday, during a somber evening meal, I was told I could begin school the following Monday. The second Monday of February, wearing clean though shabby clothes, I caught the school bus for the first time at Caledonia. The smell of cow manure went with me and I couldn't have walked too briskly. If I were shy that first day at Houston High, I had reason to be even more so on my first day at Caledonia High.

Inside the school searching for the office, I edged along the wall away from student traffic. Locating the office, I waited at the counter as the secretary worked her way through first-comes. She approached me last.

"Good morning, young man," the secretary said. "What can I do for you?" She placed both hands on the counter, stiffened her arms, and smiled.

"Uh. I'm supposed to register for school?" I said.

"I'd say you're in the right place," she said, taking pencil and paper. Her smile brightened and I felt more at ease. "I'll need your grade and former school so I can send for your transcript."

"Tenth grade," I replied, watching her write. "Houston High. Biology, English, social studies. I missed . . . maybe two months of school this year, all told. Is that all right?"

"It isn't, but if you work extra hard, you might just make it," she said. "I better write that down, Mr. Zuelke should know about that—help you catch up, that sort of thing." She handed me the paper. "Room 205, Mr. Zuelke. That'll be your homeroom; it's also biology. Things may change when we get your transcript, but this'll get you started. Mr. Zuelke is also our gym teacher and coach. Big man, hard to miss."

Knocking on the door of room 205, I waited, then stepped back as a large man filled the doorway, gazing down on me.

"Yes?"

"The office said to come . . . come here," I stammered

"Yes, of course." Mr. Zuelke took the paper. "Come in." He scanned the paper as I passed him and waited just inside the room. He murmured almost too low to hear, "Missed two months. Mmm. Could be a problem." He pointed to an empty desk. "Sit there. I'll assign someone to help you catch up."

After class, Mr. Zuelke stood alongside the door as students filed out. He reached past others and gently gripped my upper arm, pulling me alongside the door near another boy.

"Peter, this is Terry. He has agreed to help you catch up," Mr. Zuelke said. "I'll ask Gene, who's not here today, to help as well. Both are excellent students."

"Hi," Terry said, smiling broadly. "I guess we have the same classes."

"Hi," I said forcing a smile.

Terry waved himself off, "Gotta run, Peter. Call you Pete?"

"Sure, anything."

"See you in study hall, then." Terry nodded to Mr. Zuelke and disappeared.

Gene, who lived farther out on our rural route, also helped me in study hall. It was usually easy for me to catch up in the natural sciences, but biology involved more memory and research, and it seemed impossible that I could cram enough before final exams. Fortunately, John did not keep me home until fieldwork began in March, allowing me to catch up in most classes.

The last Saturday of March, as John and I prepared field

equipment near the silo, a car entered the driveway, stopped by the house, and a young woman, whom I had never met, stepped out.

"Yoo-hoo," the woman called, waving while stepping toward us.

John straightened and strode over to meet her. After conversing low with her, he faced me.

"You to come," he said, motioning.

I approached John and the woman in slow measured movement and stood aside as they faced each other.

"This Miss Angier," John said.

Looking at the ground, I glanced from John's boots to Miss Angier's shoes.

"Hello, Peter. I'm from State Social Services," she said, offering her hand.

"Hello," I said and shook her hand.

"How have you been? Miss Borsch wondered how you're making out in your new school."

"Okay, I guess," I said, staring at the ground.

"Are you sure there isn't something you want to tell me?" Miss Angier asked. A concerned look wrinkled her face and she leaned forward as though a whisper would do.

I couldn't look her in the face and wanted to scream about John and that crazy farm. Instead I just stared and mumbled at the ground. "Guess not."

She turned to John. "May I speak to Peter in my car?"

"What's he say to you, he say to me," John snapped. I didn't look, but his voice said he stared wide-eyed down the bridge of his nose at her.

"Well . . ." Miss Angier said, and paused. "Well, I see there's little to be done at this time." She extended her hand to me. "Be sure to contact me if you have any questions." She slowly got into her car, sat a moment staring through the windshield, then started the engine and drove off.

I felt depressed for days after. I did not know that Emma had been writing letters asking State Social Services to remove me immediately. Supposedly, the letters had John's blessing, but during the social worker's visit, nothing was mentioned by either Miss Angier or John. Emma remained out of sight in the house. But the visit seemed to have meant something, for John was quieter and I missed no more school before summer vacation.

Gene took biology and English with me. When Mr. Zuelke asked him to help me catch up, he did, reluctantly at first. I did not realize that my sullenness and dress would cause even the friendliest of kids to keep their distance. In the beginning, Gene and I talked on the bus, mostly about our classes. Soon, we talked about farming and our homes.

"Only a week to exams," Terry muttered. We were in study hall, Terry, Gene, and I, whispering the latest news.

"Don't remind me," Gene said. He cast a wry glance aside at Terry then faced me. "Dad can't wait 'til school's out."

"You got to work, right?" I asked.

"Yeah, but we snooze after dinner, and I go to town a lot with Mom."

"I go to church Sundays, but we go right home after," I said. "Last summer I went to town twice, besides church."

"No kidding?" Gene said. "Didn't you go to the fair?"

"Fair?" I said. "Guess not." I felt even more out of place. "Anyway, if there's dirty work—"

"You get it. Right?" Gene interrupted.

"Yeah."

"I believe you," Gene murmured. "The way Dad talks about Schauls."

"He knows him?"

"Not exactly. Our neighbor knows him. Anyway, you guys are threshing with us, so I'll see him soon enough. Not that I'm looking forward to it."

"Don't say anything to your parents," I said. "If it gets back to John, I could be dead."

"He beats on you?"

"Not much," I said, talking low. "Bitches a lot, though. Keeps repeating things—like he could write a whole book with three sentences. I'm trying to get away from him."

"Why don't you just leave?"

Gene sounded puzzled.

"Don't know," I replied. "Where would I go? It's a long story."

Gene leaned his head near mine, "I got time."

"If I don't do what they say—him and the state—seems I'd be breaking some crazy law or something," I said. "I mean, they have a paper that says Schauls and the state have to agree on it if I leave. He can beat the crap out of me, but I'd probably go to jail in Red Wing for leaving him. Whatcha gonna do?"

"That don't make sense, the state telling you what to do here in Caledonia," Gene whispered. "Besides, the court decides who goes to Red Wing."

"I'm a state ward," I said. "They're the court. I'm in this mess because they couldn't find a better place for me. If they can't find a decent home for a state ward, they give him to a farmer. Good-looking white kids get decent homes."

"Schauls got you because you're Indian, right?"

I shrugged.

We studied biology until the end of the hour. As we got up to leave, my chair was knocked from behind and an elbow jabbed the back of my neck.

"Oh, so sorry, Injun," the boy snarled. He moved on sneering over his shoulder at me.

I stared at the boy's back.

"Know him?" Terry asked.

"No," I replied. "Should I?"

"He knows you," Gene said. "Biggest bully in school."

"Don't know how many times they kicked him out of school for drinking and bullying," Terry said. He appeared disgusted as he watched the boy leave. "Mostly picks on small guys."

I nodded.

"He pesters smaller guys into fighting then kills them," Gene said. "Take you. He thinks there's no one on your side. Ten to one, 'cause you're skinny, he'll make you fight him."

"Why me?" I asked.

"He's Bud Lange."

"Our landlord's son?" I said. "No wonder Schauls gets along with them. How old is he?"

"Eighteen and a lot of months," Gene said. "Looked the same since grade school."

Though a bully roamed the halls of Caledonia High, a teacher named Mr. Zuelke shared good thoughts when I needed them most. He stood in the hall as students moved between classes. One day, he stepped into my path and held his arm up, stopping me.

"Good afternoon, Peter," he said. A toothpick flagged out of the right side of his mouth as he talked. "Think you could go out for track and football?" He then looked over my head and about the hall.

"I'd like to, but I have to work," I said.

"Other farm boys take part in sports," he insisted.

"I mean, my guardian won't even let me go to games and things," I said. "Besides, I couldn't ask him."

Mr. Zuelke sighed and removed the toothpick. "Well, if things change, let me know. I'd like to see you out for track." He looked down at my feet. "I noticed that you have no tennis shoes for gym, and your gym shorts are small for you. Does your guardian—Schauls, isn't it—plan to get those for you?"

"Maybe not. I don't have any money."

"See me at noon," Mr. Zuelke said, matter-of-fact. "I might have shorts and shoes in your size."

"I can't pay for them," I said.

"Not to worry. People outgrow and donate things and we give them to others," Mr. Zuelke said, holding the toothpick near his mouth, then stuck it in his lips.

Fieldwork continued. Though I was no longer kept home from school that spring, bringing studies to the farm was like touching fire to gasoline so I did all homework in study hall. Final exams were only moderately difficult, though I worried that I had failed something. All exam scores but biology were posted on the hall bulletin board, and those students waited in study hall until Mr. Zuelke would post them.

Terry, Gene, others, and I whispered at one table in study hall.

"Wonder why biology scores aren't posted," I said.

Gene shrugged, "Who knows?"

"Shhhh, here comes Zuelke now," a boy whispered.

"Good morning, people," Mr. Zuelke said. "Would you like to know who passed my favorite subject?" He looked over our heads about the room while probing delicately with a toothpick through closed lips.

"You passed," Mr. Zuelke said pointing to Gene, Terry, and others, then to girls at the next table. He made the rounds of the study hall, addressing all biology students but me. About to leave the room, he paused in the doorway looking out at the hall floor as though struggling through a quandary.

Gene leaned toward me. "He forgot you," he whispered.

"Nope," I whispered back. "I flunked and he didn't want to say so in public."

Mr. Zuelke spun around in the doorway and faced our table, the toothpick no longer in his mouth. His eyes smiled.

"Peter, you had the highest A in the class." He spoke louder than he had to the other students, then left without another word.

I was thrilled but dared not show any emotion.

"Good going, Pete," said Gene's sister Kathy on her way to the door.

"Holy cow," Terry said, "Sure you didn't cheat?"

I flushed, "Don't they keep State Board exams in Fort Knox until test time?" I said, smiling. "But it has to be wrong."

"Zuelke *never* makes mistakes," Gene said.

We went to find that biology scores were now posted and

that I had, indeed, gotten the highest grade. Mr. Zuelke's announcement, I learned, was a lesson to students whom he had overheard making snide remarks about my race and my threadbare clothes. The test moved my final biology grade from near failing to a C average. I was promoted to eleventh grade.

7

I had never seen Dr. Yager in the cottage until, one evening, he entered the day room of c-16 carrying a cloth bag. Boys were reading, playing cards, or listening to the radio. Dr. Yager looked right at me.

"Would you like to play checkers?" he asked. He slid the contents of the bag out onto an unused table.

"Checkers—with you?" I stammered.

"If you don't mind," Dr. Yager said. His smile firmed, but didn't seem genuine. He set up the board.

"You may have the first move, Peter," Dr. Yager of-
fered. He extended an upturned palm generously
over the board.

I shifted uneasily in my seat, wondering why the
school psychologist wanted to play checkers with
me. Dr. Yager never did anything without an ulterior
motive, to read a boy's body language or lull him
long enough to trick him into revealing something
secret. I moved a checker, watching Dr. Yager's strat-
egy more than planning my own. I didn't like the
other boys watching and sat with my head leaning
on one hand and let my hair hang over my face.
Though my first moves might have seemed clever,
I lost.

. . .

During a work-lull between haying and cultivating that summer, I thought John would give me an extra half-day off. Instead, he sent me to a neighboring farm where I worked two
eight-hour days and still did all my chores at home. I didn't
like being hired out, but the farmer fed me well, and we talked
about things other than farming. Two weeks later, the farmer,
who attended our church, pulled me aside after Mass.

"Did you get the twenty bucks?" he asked. "I gave it to
John."

My surprise left me speechless, but I should have guessed.
As with my summer wages, my trust fund and the money I
saved for a bicycle, John had stolen the wages I was owed for
those two days. I sensed the farmer knew that I would not get
the money, but he wanted me to know who had robbed me. It

didn't do any good. I was afraid to argue with John, so I said nothing.

When threshing time came, I went to Gene's farm while John was in town. With John along, I would have said little to anyone and only whispered to Gene. With him gone, however, the work seemed easier, and I talked and joked with Gene and another boy. Gene and I tended the granary until Paul, Gene's father, brought in the last wagon of grain bundles before lunch. We stood there shirtless, our bodies covered with grain dust and streaked by sweat, when Gene's mother, Florence, called from the house porch.

"Come and get it or go hungry!"

"Coming!" Paul yelled. He handed Gene the reins to his team of horses. "Time to eat, boys." He pointed at us while smiling, "After you water and feed the horses, rinse off at the stock tank. Florence expects T-shirts and clean hands and faces at the table." No sooner did Paul turn toward the house, than I was hit in the back with a stream of icy water.

"I'll help you wash," Gene yelled.

I grappled with Gene for the hose. We laughed and splashed with an abandon I would never have shown at the Schaulses'. If for only the moment, I was free from John's glare. Another call came from the house.

"Boys! Are you eatin' with us or not?" Florence called.

"Coming!" Gene yelled as we shook water from our hair. Our play had rinsed us off and we had only to don T-shirts as we headed to the house.

After dinner, Florence served desserts. Gene asked his father, "When's the party at Thorsons'?"

"Couple weeks. Why?"

"Pete can, may come, can't he?" Gene asked, glancing at me.

"Why not? It's open house," Florence interjected. She smiled to firm up the invitation. "You might like it. Give you a break from work."

"That might be good," I said. Such pleasures, commonplace to some, were almost more than I could hope for. "I'll plan on it."

I approached John during milking Thursday evening, "There's a dance party at Thorson's, Friday," I said. "Maybe I'll go. . . . After chores, I mean."

"We's to work Saturday," John said. "If you tired, maybe you don't to earn wages. It important we earns our way."

"I'll come home early; just wanted to see Gene again before sch—" I caught myself. "I wanted to see Gene again."

John's eyes flashed with his displeasure, but he hadn't been drinking so he said little.

When Friday evening's chores were finally done, I dressed in my threadbare school clothes and headed to the Thorson farm. The walk was over a mile in the dark, but I focused on the glow from the Thorson's windows, and the thought of seeing friends urged me on.

My knock was answered by Mrs. Thorson, who ushered me into a roomful of smiles and warm conversation. I was more at ease than at my first 4-h meeting. Leaning against a wall of the large living room, I was mesmerized by a scene of red-faced farmers and their wives dancing and smiling. It was the first time since listening to a folk singer at the State School that I was so enthralled by live music.

Gene approached with two glasses of beer. "Pete, old boy," he said, his broad grin enhanced by earlier consumption. He shoved a beer at me while holding the other near his mouth. "Have one."

I shot a glance at Gene's mother who sipped a red drink while talking with other women. "Your ma lets you drink beer?" I tried to hide surprise. "We're not old enough."

"We're all seventeen, aren't we?"

"Yeah, seventeen," I agreed. "But we're supposed to be twenty-one. Aren't we?

"Who's going to raid this place?" Gene said. He swigged his beer and waved it near me. "So we're old enough! Anyway, I never get drunk."

"Never been drunk, huh?" I said, cautiously sipping the beer.

Gene watched me closely, "Dad says one or two don't hurt."

I looked over at Paul drinking beer with other farmers. "Thanks," I said, then gestured with the glass. "Good stuff."

"Yeah, sure," Gene teased. "You didn't even know what it tasted like."

"So what," I said. "Knew the smell—John's a walking beer glass."

"Nah," Gene said. "Talk is, he drinks whiskey."

"Could be," I agreed.

Kathy approached. "Oh, hello, Peter," she said, smiling. She was an amazing sight—beautiful and sixteen.

"Hi, Kathy," I said, blushing. I could have melted into the wall.

Kathy turned to Gene. "Mom wants you to run home, get some bread and that sandwich meat in the fridge."

"Hey, that's over a quarter mile," Gene complained, "You do it."

"Want me to tell Dad." Her voice was vaguely threatening.

"I'll go with you," I said to Gene.

"No, you won't," a familiar voice called from behind me. A hand gripped my shoulder, turned me around, and I found myself poised to dance with Florence.

"Maybe I shouldn't dance. My knee, you know," I said, favoring it for emphasis.

"Wasn't going to bother you running to our house," she said smiling. "And I'd say you looked healthy enough threshing, too."

"Well, you see, it's all right for walking and running and that, but dancing . . . well, twists it."

Florence pressed, "I suppose your knee would suddenly feel better if Katherine asked you to dance."

"You know, I could try," I said. "And it's kind of you to ask, but I just can't dance."

"I'll help you," Florence said, and before I knew it, she had pulled my hand around her waist and shuffled with me to slow music. As we danced, I observed Gene heading out the door and Kathy helping with refreshments. Other women danced with me, then Kathy, but I was glad we stopped before I ruined all their shoes.

I returned home at midnight, flushed with excitement.

I only got haircuts during school noon-hour at Houston High, so my hair grew thick and long over summer. It was the same at Caledonia. Emma seldom concerned herself with my appearance unless it served another purpose. Summer was almost gone. John prepared to get feed in town, which meant—most certainly—that he would tie one on.

"Take Peter so he gets his hair cut," Emma said. "I haint going to have folks say he lives here, lookin' like that."

It puzzled me then why Emma suddenly noticed my hair, but I now know that she wanted me along so John would have to come home for chores.

"He's to works when I's in town," John began, then looked at my hair and relented. "You to help me with feed in town." I turned toward the house to get my school clothes. "You wear those clothes," John said. He motioned me to the passenger side as he settled into the driver's seat. Having no pickup, John hauled everything in the back seat of the 1934 Ford, or had it delivered. After I helped John at the feed mill, he dropped me off at the barbershop. "Come to Shanty Bar when you hair done," John said, pointing.

Finished with my trimming, I walked to the Shanty Bar. I saw John leaning over the bar, his back to the entrance. I slid against the wall near the door and looked around, waiting. Two men occupied stools at the bar, and a man and woman sat at a table. They were all either older than John or smaller.

John looked over his shoulder at me and his eyes flashed. I stiffened nervously as he tilted his head back and glared slowly around at the other patrons. "I can lick anyone in des house!" he called out.

I thought I was about to be caught in the crossfire of a bar fight, but one man just squinted at John, then calmly sipped his beer as though John weren't there. No one else paid him any attention. I relaxed when no one accepted his challenge, but John was clearly pleased. He hoisted his glass with overdone flourishes and drank with his head cocked back, his nose high like royalty.

Days before school started, John came home with his hat pulled low. He said nothing during chores. While washing equipment after milking, John's cap brushed back revealing a badly bruised face with one eye half closed and purple. I remained stone-faced and was careful to avoid him until bedtime, but I was secretly glad to know that someone had put him in his place.

He drank more after that night, and he was agitated all the time. Emma's tension increased, and she became openly nervous. Monday after breakfast, I boarded the school bus to begin my junior year. There were no comments, good or bad, from the Schaulses, but I felt cold eyes follow me to the bus.

John said little against school the first week, but an eerie tension permeated the house at supper, Friday, the second week of school. John was not home, which worried me most. In stocking feet and T-shirt, I washed for supper after doing early chores alone. It seemed obvious that Emma, beset by fear, had tangled with John while I was in school.

Soon, a car stopped in the driveway and its door slammed shut. Emma fussed uselessly at the stove. I knew something was going on, but I didn't know what. I suddenly had the fear that John might kill me. My stomach knotted.

The door opened and John entered. Unsteady, he moved to sit at the table. "Supper ready?" he yelled.

"It's coming," Emma said. She set a plate before me, one near John, then set food dishes on the table.

"You drink too much," Emma said. "Who knows when youse is comin' home."

She slid a food dish across the table toward John.

John shoved his chair back and stood. "You to keep mouth shut, woman!"

As they glared at each other, I tried to move around John toward the door, but before I could escape, John punched my chest. I flew into Emma and we both stumbled. I straightened, pulled Emma erect and leapt around John toward the door. Near the washbasin, I grabbed my shoes, barn clothes, and jerked the door open. Moving through the doorway with my hand still on the knob, I heard a sickening thud. Without stopping, I glanced backward. That image remains crystal clear:

Emma is frozen in the air, stiffened and falling backward, arms straight by her sides. Her glasses are suspended above her head and John's fist still follows her face.

John had shoved Emma in front of me, but I had not before seen him strike her with a closed fist. I wanted to stop and help her, but I wasn't strong enough to fight a grown man, not John, not in one of his rages. I ran out to the barn.

Half an hour passed. I milked my cows and my stomach ached. When John entered, he was still strutting with his head back, glaring down his nose. Violence seemed to intoxicate him as much as alcohol. I had no supper that night. Instead, I stayed in the barn and ate soybean meal and other animal feed.

I did not see Emma for days after the beating. John fried eggs, made simple meals the first two days, and breakfast was on the table after milking the third morning. Emma prepared subsequent meals, but would not show herself. Four days passed before I saw her, and even then she was quiet, doing her work with a blank expression. I felt sorry for her. I knew what it was like to suffer such violent attacks.

Though c-16 was much better than c-15, I had to work outside the cottage during my thirteenth summer for Mr. Beaty. On hot, sticky days, we still waited until Mr. Beaty decided it was time for water or shade. It didn't matter how the sun burned, he stood with crossed arms daring certain ones to complain. No one dared.

"He's tough but fair," Percy said.

"He treats me okay," Ted said.

He knew gardening, but Mr. Beaty was like a guard supervising hard labor. He spent many years working for Superintendent Merril before I arrived at Owatonna. Under Merril, who had been an Army officer, non-cottage employees were called guards. Discipline was severe. A boy at the school during the nineteen twenties, whom I later met, was beaten—caned—on the back so severely, he bore scars for life. The boy was an Indian.

Although conditions improved under Mr. Mendus Vevle, who took over about the time I arrived, it was slowed by a matronage accustomed to the penal philosophy of child rearing. I heard from Roy and others, how Mr. Beaty attacked George Lawson in the garden. It seemed to take weeks before George healed. George was black. Although Mr. Beaty was respected by many youths and staff of a mostly white institution, my strongest lessons from him were about the dark side of man.

Boys went off to work one day to the Main Building, the barns, and gardens. Dale, Allen, and I were among those heading to the gardens. Mr. Beaty dispensed weeding scrapers and gave orders as boys straggled up to him. When speaking to Allen—"Over there, weed the strawberries"—he was firm but calm. His attitude changed when he spoke to Dale, and he only spoke to me through him. "Weed the beans. Make the lazy Injun do his share. Get some work out of that thing for a change." And his eyes burned the words deeper. Fuming, I began weeding a row adjacent to Dale.

Beaty treats you better than me," I said.

"Think so?" Dale asked. "Maybe he's strict, or you could be right about him having it against coloreds, the way he nearly killed Portz that time. Lawson, too, I guess."

"Yeah," I muttered. "Musta hit him hard enough to break his paddle. When he paddled me, I couldn't sit decent for weeks."

We knelt between rows, propped on one hand, weeding with the other. Mr. Beaty came by, stood behind us with his hands clasped behind his back and legs spread. I was relieved when he moved to watch others.

With Mr. Beaty out of sight, I could relax. Joking as we weeded, I laughed at something Dale said and accidentally cut a bean plant off. I looked to my right nervously. Seeing no one, I was about to look left when something struck me violently from behind. I sprawled on my stomach, ruining dozens of plants.

"Dirty Injun bastard!"

Mr. Beaty had kicked me in the lower back, violently wrenching my spine. I tried to lift myself from the dirt, but I was too numb from the waist down. He kicked me again, with his heavy boot, this time against my chest. Unable to catch my breath or feel my legs to stand, I could only claw at the ground. I braced myself for another kick.

"Damn it!" Dale yelled, leaping between Mr. Beaty and me. "You can't do that!"

Mr. Beaty froze.

He looked at Dale. "What?" he said. He had been off somewhere. Mr. Beaty left muttering to himself.

I rolled onto my back, staring at a blue sky with scattered puffy clouds. In spite of intense heat, I felt numb, shivering oddly and turned my head to keep the sun from my eyes. My breathing, gasps at first, slowly became steady.

"Cripes, Pete," Dale said, "he's raving mad."

"Always . . . was," I gasped. I tried to draw deep breaths, but my ribs hurt. "Bastard."

"Can you move?" Dale asked. He knelt near me. "You don't look good, like you're pale through the brown."

"Hope nothing's bleeding inside," I said. "Can't move my legs yet. It doesn't hurt, but I feel sleepy."

"Better get help, get you to the cottage or anyplace but here," Dale said. He stood glaring at Mr. Beaty's back.

"You better get to work," I gasped.

"Not on your life," Dale said. "He's crazy, if you ask me, but he knows it's wrong. I'm going with you."

"You know when your leg goes to sleep, like when you lay or sit wrong?" I asked. "If that's what's wrong, I should feel things pretty soon."

"I don't know." Dale sounded doubtful. "Okay, just lie still." A few minutes passed and deep aching throbs began in my upper legs, then pain seared where the first kick jammed my spine. Relieved when my face flushed, I no longer felt like sleeping, but it was fifteen minutes before I could stand.

Dale helped me up, and I took a few steps. The pain was no worse walking, so I short-stepped out of the garden to the gym lawn where I lay flat to rest and moan. Making no effort to stop us, Mr. Beaty disappeared before we left the garden.

Hunched, tilted to one side, my lower spine felt severely injured, my ribs bruised. I ached all over but managed to make my way to the Main Building where I again rested. It usually took me five minutes to walk from the garden to the cottage, but that day it took almost an hour. Arriving at the cottage, I lay across seat lockers, adjusted myself for the least pain in my back and immediately dozed off.

"My goodness Peter," Mrs. Cory said. She was bending over me as I opened my eyes. "Dale says Mr. Beaty kicked you quite hard. Is that right?"

"Yeah. It hurts," I said.

"I know the men sometimes slap boys, but it's hard to believe Mr. Beaty would almost cripple you."

"It hurts," I repeated.

"Are you sure you didn't fall and make it worse?" Mrs. Cory pressed.

"Whadaya mean?" I said. "I was already on the ground. How the heck could I fall?"

"Pete was weeding on hands and knees and Beaty kicked him over ten feet," Dale insisted. "Hard anyhow."

Mrs. Cory checked the rib bruise but seemed uncertain.

"I could send you for a check up, but if you're not bleeding, they might not do anything. You can stay near the cottage to see if it gets worse; meanwhile, I'll see if other boys are being kicked."

"Mr. Beaty called Pete a *dirty Injun Bastard*," Dale said.

"Mind your tongue!" Mrs. Cory barked.

"It's all right if Beaty says it, ain't it?" Dale shouted.

Mrs. Cory softened, "Mr. Beaty is well respected, and I'm sure he didn't intentionally hurt you."

"Sure," I mumbled. I lay flat, knees up, shifting to ease the pain in my back and covered my face with my forearm. "All I know is, it hurts like heck and Beaty done it."

"For now I'm putting you on sick restriction until further notice. I'll have a pillow for you at meal time." She turned to Dale, "Could you get a wet towel for Peter's bruises?"

"S'pose," Dale said, smirking at me. "Who was his nurse maid last year?"

My lower spine felt severely injured, and my ribs were bruised. I hurt all over. Mrs. Cory organized cottage medical restrictions with no further question. I sat on the edges of chairs for the first two weeks, then did light work away from the cottage. My ribs were sore for a week, but my back injury prevented normal bending and lifting for a month.

Mrs. Cory had to have said something. Mr. Beaty never touched me again, but I was never told that, and his specter still hung over me like a teetering deadfall. More time would pass before I knew for sure that no staff would touch me.

I almost enjoyed late fall of my thirteenth year and early winter of my fourteenth year. Although I worked amid strict discipline, it was not for the gardener, and life became a comfortable succession of days and months. However, a gnawing anxiety—perhaps suppressed at c-3 and c-15 by the treatment that caused it—prevented me from fully appreciating staff tolerance at c-16.

During leisure, I read more. We went to Wednesday evening movies at the auditorium and, on weekends, to movies in town or open gym. When deemed worthy by staff, we could sign out and go elsewhere on campus.

Though boys appreciated being on their own after work, that often exposed younger boys to bullies who constantly prowled for victims. Many boys were brought to the school late in childhood, though none after age fifteen. Of those brought after age ten, some were street wanderers who thought nothing of stealing or bullying. I feared no one my age, but I learned to be wary of certain older, bigger boys.

When winter work was done, boys circulated about the cottage or outside in mild weather. Physical activities—boxing, tag, hide and seek—were in the basement, quiet games were in the living room. The basement was spacious enough so that a pair of boys could be ignored by others.

As Roy and I sat talking on the basement seat lockers one evening, he yawned, then frowned, as two bigger boys sauntered in from the hall.

"We got visitors," Roy muttered to me. A scan of the room confirmed that we were alone with the bullies.

My chest tightened. I stood and started toward the door with Roy behind me. "Hi, Len, John. We're going upstairs," I said with unsteady machismo. As we tried to sidle past them, the bullies grabbed us.

"They're goin' to put us out," Roy muttered.

"They won't hurt us, will they?" I managed, twisting in John's grasp.

"We wouldn't think of hurtin' ya," John sneered. He was a soft sixteen-year-old of medium build. Lenard was thinner, taller than John—a follower who bullied little on his own. He helped capture victims while John decided the method of torture.

"You don't have to hold so tight," Roy complained.

"Yeah, you're hurting," I said.

"Don't move and it won't hurt," John said. "Off with the T-shirts."

"Bullshit! It's cold down here," I said, my voice quivering. Roy removed his T-shirt.

"Hold Pete, I'll get his shirt off," John said.

Forcing Roy deep into the corner, they turned on me, stripping my T-shirt from me.

"Klein's going to bitch about that," I said, as the T-shirt tore.

"That's your problem," John said. His voice was hoarse like Mr. Beaty's. "Off with your pants. Or do we take them off?"

Roy grumbled and dropped his pants, standing sullenly in shorts and bare feet.

"What is this?" I asked. "Why the pants?"

John punched me in the side of the head. I moaned.

"Then shut yer trap," he said. John held my shoulders from behind, as I removed my shoes and pants. Once my pants were off, I felt sudden pressure on my neck and chest, then everything went black.

I awoke shaking from the cold. The bullies were gone.

It wasn't clear what they did to us. I remember thinking, *At least, my shorts are on*. Roy was quivering too. He awoke just as my hand touched his head.

"You hurting anyplace?" I asked.

"Don't know," he mumbled. He raised himself onto one knee then stood. "Did they let us fall?"

"Maybe not," I said. My fear turned to anger as we dressed. I started ranting on our way up to the living room. "They did that to you before, huh? How long would you say we slept? They do that to other guys? Does Cory know about this? Let's get a bunch of guys and gang up on them."

"Bastards," Roy muttered.

"Dirty turds," I said. We paused on the landing.

I looked at Roy. "What'd they do to us, Roy?"

"Who knows?" Roy whispered. "Cory says I'm gonna get big, like over six feet. Hope it's before them s.o.b.s leave. I'll beat the shit out of them."

We went to the dorm, undressed and climbed into our adjacent beds, talking to comfort each other until we slept.

By the time the Schaulses moved to Caledonia, the State Public School was a closed orphanage, and social workers came out of St. Paul to check on state wards. Expecting a visit from a social worker, John allowed me to attend school until silo filling, then he kept me home from school a full week. Gene didn't lose school for work, not even when we filled their silo.

Back in school, English and social studies were easy to make up. Missing a week of chemistry, however, meant hard work in study hall. Other boys, Gene, and I were at a study hall table my first day back in school.

I whispered to Gene across the table, "Did I miss anything in chemistry last week?" I opened my text. "While I filled your silo?"

"Just the most important chapter, is all," Gene replied, smirking. "It ain't my fault you miss school for work. Anyway, we were supposed to sketch a Martian molecule."

"Which one?" I asked with a straight face. "Red sand or the green blood of little creatures?"

"A Martian girl's breath." Gene smiled.

I laughed then became serious. "Hey, Gene, know any farmers who need chore and Saturday help during winter?"

"I'll fill you in on last week's work on the bus," Gene said soberly. "Live there, too, right?"

"Yeah," I said, "I got to get away from Schauls. He's driving me crazy."

"Yeah, my dad says the Schaulses are odd, but it's mostly the old man, sounds like," Gene said. "If he's doing those things, you gotta get away. How's Emma after John KO'd her?"

"Doesn't say much. She's different though," I said. "Musta had a bad concussion, I think it's called."

"Yeah, that's what my dad calls it," Gene said. "I had one once, Mom says. Hit my head on a beam in the hay mow."

"Knock you out?" I asked, smirking, "Or crack the beam?"

"Na, just kinda dizzy for a couple days, smart ass. Had a funny headache too. You ever have one?"

"Wouldn't call them funny, but yeah, sure did," I said. I became nervous again. "Anyway, if I'm ever going to get through high school in one piece, I gotta leave. Lucky to pass tenth grade. Guess I'm old enough to be a hired hand."

8

Not weekly or even monthly, but every couple of months, usually on a Sunday afternoon, married couples strolled through the cottage living room. During such visits we were encouraged to be on our best behavior with no boisterous activities. My naive thought was that they were hunting for kids, but before meeting children, couples were guided by office staff through files heavy with matron's notes. A boy would never see the assistant point him out from a distance or through a door. That's him, there.

A boy never knew when or how the decision was made. A formally dressed couple might simply stroll through the sitting room, smile for everyone and stop, almost too casually, near him. They would talk in low voices, and shortly the boy would stand, look at Mrs. Cory who nodded, and leave with the visiting couple. In less than two weeks that boy had a new family and a new name.

. . .

"You're working far below your potential," the principal said. I had been called into her office at Caledonia High to discuss my academic performance. "Your teachers think that if you work harder, you could go to college on a scholarship, especially in the sciences."

"It'd be all right," I replied, "but I don't have time for study at home, and I have only one study period."

"It's a shame," the principal said. "I understand you're in a foster home. I just wanted to tell you that you could do it if you wanted to."

"Thanks," I said. Returning to classes, I was briefly elated that someone thought I could be more than a farmhand. The euphoria faded as I wondered how I could break clean from John. When I was fourteen, I had tried to run away from the State School. The experience left me wary of being on my own until I knew exactly where I was going.

During the spring when I was fourteen, I started growing restless at the State School. During recreation, I headed to a junkyard off campus, scouring the woods. Other times I would walk the tracks alone, wondering about trains, cities, and mountains, or would tromp out into the fields, watching insects, or birds building nests in the bushes. Curiosity drove my pastimes.

In the classroom, with my head on the desk, I often stared sideways out the window where everything looked warm and cozy. Teachers seemed to admonish me less, leaving me daydreaming at the rear of the classroom until they could stand it no longer.

The teacher whispered my name near my desk. She had been walking down the aisle, which I didn't notice, handing papers back with usual comments.

I sat erect, peering through hair draped over my eyes.

"Peter!" she repeated. "Don't you sleep at the cottage?" She laid a paper on a nearby student's desk. "The class did well on the test. How some students pass without studying is beyond me." While sliding a paper in front of me, she said, "You earned an A in spelling and English. I knew you could do it. You're just mentally lazy."

Another day, the teacher caught me whispering across the aisle. "Your hand on the desk, palm up," she said, brandishing, not a ruler, but a stout yardstick. I lay my hand on the desk and slowly opened my palm as she raised the yardstick high over her head.

It might have been her sudden movement or the way she grunted—like being jabbed in the abdomen—whatever it was, I jerked my hand back before she whacked it. The yardstick shattered on the desk, reduced to splinters scattered about the floor. Embarrassed, I'm certain, for exposing the viciousness of her intended punishment—like Mrs. Burt with the broken brooms—the teacher gathered the pieces and stomped back to her desk as soft laughter rippled through the classroom.

This nervous energy often made me careless. Early April 1943, was unusually warm even for south central Minnesota. I was running barefoot through brown grass from the previous autumn, when something seemed to catch my foot, and I fell face down. Laying on my stomach, I twisted to see two inches of rake tine protruding from my upper foot, the skin bleached around the point. Then blood oozed out around the tine. I lay there staring, waiting, until a boy, who was nearby, pulled the rake out. He helped me as I hopped fifty yards to the hospital where I grimaced through a series of four tetanus shots. The wound was bad enough that they wanted to keep me in the hospital for a while.

Paul, in the bed next to me, wore a full cast on his leg to the hip. A year older than me, very thin with light hair, he had come to the State School only two years before. He was a freshman in high school and decades ahead of me in understanding the real world. We were both alert and began talking soon after I was in bed.

"I bummed around the streets a lot when I was thirteen," Paul began. "That'd be two years ago. Then some goof got the bright idea to send me here."

"Were you scared?" I asked.

"Pissed off," he said, squirming to sit higher in bed. "But it ain't so bad. Here at the school, I mean, not counting this damn accident. Remember when you got here?"

"Can't remember," I said. "What about it?"

"Well, the county guy bringing me here stops in this old store for cigarettes. So's I don't run off, he takes me in the store with him. When he turns his back, I hid behind shelves, and snuck out the back door."

"But you're here," I said.

"Yeah, that's just it. The old coot was waiting when I came out."

"They're sneaky all right," I said with half a smile. "What happened to your leg? Or is it your hip?"

"Worst damn thing I ever did," Paul replied. "I pumps the bicycle into that alley near the hotel, you know."

I interrupted, "You got a bicycle?"

"Jees, where you been?" Paul rolled his eyes at the ceiling.

"Here."

"Maybe that's it," Paul said with a sigh. "Besides, it weren't my bike. It belonged to the telegraph office. Anyway, I go lickety-split into the alley just as a pickup truck comes from the other end. I remember trying to stop, but the bumper shoved me down and," he hesitated as though the memory itself was painful, "the truck runs over me. I figure I'm dying and everything goes black. Nothing. Next thing, I know, I wake up under the truck, which is jacked up, and they're cutting the bike apart."

"Did you break your leg bad?" I asked.

"Crushed the upper bone," Paul said. "Been here six months already and Doc says I'll be here more months."

I limped to the cottage after two days, didn't have to work for a week, but was ordered to wear tennis shoes for another two weeks.

Exploration at c-15 was limited to the cottage and playground, but at c-16, boys often went AWOL into town or for some distance along the railroad track. The c-16 staff was not inclined to notice those brief campaigns so long as boys arrived on time at work and meals. My excursions into the nearby world were a combination of excitement and fear, as I inched further out into a world unknown to me, a world of cities larger than Owatonna and places I only knew about through movies.

My curiosity and growing restlessness struck a chord with Dale and Chuck. We talked one day about the Waseca outing, then about problems we had with staff and bullies. Dale arrived at the State School when he was seven, shortly after his mother died, and understood far more about the world outside than me. His older sister worked in the main building and was well liked. Employees were reluctant to more than berate Dale for fear of official repercussion, but Dale was witness to many incidents of staff cruelty. Chuck seemed more afraid than Dale and complained bitterly about older bullies.

"We should just go," Chuck said finally.

Bullies picked on him constantly. We were his only friends, and he was willing to risk it. We decided there was no time like the present to strike off on our own. It was slightly overcast, not too hot, and that which couldn't be seen or imagined beckoned stronger than hot meals or snug beds. Within moments of first discussing it, we were walking west on the tracks and didn't look back. We had no idea where to go or how to get there.

"This'll get us jam and maybe three loaves of bread," Chuck said, counting our coins that amounted to one dollar and fifteen cents.

We spent the next two nights and three days with mosquitoes and poor water. We slept on the hard ground without covers. Though Chuck got us a lawn trimming job in Waseca, Dale and he became ill, leaving me with most of the work. Nevertheless, we each got thirty-five cents. On the third morning, we woke on the beach, rinsed in Clear Lake, then went into a small lake-front store to buy food. Little did we know, the clerk had already called the sheriff. When Chuck finished paying for our bread and jam, the door opened and two huge deputies entered and herded us away to the sheriff's office where Mr. Doleman would pick us up. The store clerk kept the groceries and our money.

From the Records of the State School, April 1943:

Miss Putter received a telephone call from Mrs. Parker, welfare board, Waseca, executive secretary, that boys apparently from the school were boarding themselves on the lake shore in Waseca. Miss Putter asked Mrs. Parker to notify the Waseca county sheriff to pick them up and that they would be called for.

[LATER]

Worker was notified by Miss Putter, who called the sheriff's office and learned the boys had been picked up and were there. He called for them and returned them to the school.

There seemed to be no object for their going except to have good a time. They had no definite destination and had gone west and south to Meridan, Hartland, Richland Center, then up to Waseca.

The day following our return, I was sent to the hospital beset by diarrhea, 104° fever and severe dehydration. Miss Plum and the doctor were concerned during the first days.

"Must have been the runaway," Miss Pearl suggested.

The hospital staff was as pleased as me when, after eight days, fully recovered, I returned to c-16.

Back at the cottage, staff seemed to have forgotten my running away. They didn't even mind that I was still such good friends with Dale and a new boy named Billy, who arrived at the school shortly after I transferred to c-16. He was not my friend the way Dale was, but he had few other friends and seemed comfortable with Dale and me. His apparent adjustment to the State School was probably closer to helpless acceptance of something he really couldn't understand—like I couldn't understand the world from which he just came. Soft-spoken, often almost to whispering, he seemed to shield his deeper thoughts, and, like me, he was incapable of exuberance.

July turned hotter, and our impatience grew, so Dale and I decided to run away again. Billy asked to join us, confiding that relatives in St. Paul might take him if we got that far. Dale and I agreed. Little of our brief excursion to Waseca made sense to me, but I realized that planning was needed were I to make it on my own. That expedition taught me a lesson that was never, in any form, taught at the State School—how to plan for myself. The State School fed, clothed, and sheltered us, allowing little choice of work or activities outside of free time, which was confined to specific areas. The staff always claimed, *It's for your own good.* Almost every decision I tried to make for myself seemed inappropriate amid strict schedules.

All three of us, each for our own reasons, began preparations on the last Monday in July to run away that Friday night after last bed check. Studying maps of Minnesota in the library, I also scanned maps of the entire country—just in case. The maps seemed clear enough, but my vision of such a trip was shrouded in mist and the more I planned, the hazier things became.

Monday night, Roy and I talked briefly in the dorm, though I mentioned nothing about our trip. We were sworn to secrecy. I fell asleep thinking of the reservation in northern Minnesota, wondering how one could possibly get to a place so far away.

The faint moan of a train whistle tugged me awake. While I stared at the ceiling, it blew again, closer. I rolled onto my side and cocked my head to listen. Beginning with a soft moan, the whistle reached crescendo with an eerie wail before fading mournfully. The rumbling and chugging grew louder and the soft wheezing of venting steam drifted through the open window as the train slowed. Never quite ceasing, the rumbling was interrupted by a staccato roar as the driving wheels spun. The train accelerated north out of town, and I fell asleep thinking how at least we might begin our journey.

An east-west track went past the cottage playground. The north-south track, the one we wanted, was farther in town. I stayed awake Tuesday night to confirm that the train did indeed go north at midnight. It did. There was magic in that forlorn sound. A call to adventure—like Jack London's *Call of the Wild*. Standing just inside the bedroom door, I watched the hall clock while timing the chugs.

Wednesday, timing the chugs of a westbound freight past the school, I was able to guess how fast the midnight freight traveled at its slowest. We would have ten seconds to get aboard, I reasoned. If we ran a little.

Thursday morning, Dale confirmed the passage of the northbound freight the previous night. I was in constant fear that someone would discover our plan. One of the snitches would find out and turn us in, or staff might collar us at work or recreation. Dale and I slid furtively through a window of the Main Building food stores while Billy raided the clothing room for clean shirts and underwear. We packed everything in an old suitcase, which we stashed under the old arched, wood bridge over the railroad. It seemed we had everything necessary to be on our own. A knife, flashlight, four cans of Spam, two loaves of bread, two bottles of jam and clean clothes. Knowing about farm chores, lawn work, and house cleaning, we hoped such work would get us started.

The weather began to warm Wednesday and, by Friday, Owatonna sweltered in ninety-five degree heat, which dropped little after dark. The heat was stifling in the c-16 dorms. Boys slept atop covers in their briefs; I was wet as if I had just stepped from a shower. Though tired, I was too nervous to fall asleep and lay counting down the hours.

Long branches of the cottonwood trees nearly brushed our dorm windows. Other nights I had stared at the branches flickering hypnotically in the streetlight glow, their rustle and sway often lulling me to sleep. That night, however, no breeze moved through the open windows or sighed among the branches. Miss Klein's bed-check itinerary never varied, nor did her quiet shoes normally awaken us. She began the last

bed check in Dale's dorm, went through ours, finally returning to her room for the night.

Later, near the exterior door, we each wore denims, a
T-shirt and low-cut tennis shoes without socks. To prevent
suspicion, we had kept only everyday clothes by our beds,
storing all other clothes in the suitcase. We slipped into the
shadow of the cottage created by the streetlight. Dale led the
way into the bushes but Billy stood stunned. I nudged him,
questioning the wisdom of having him along. But we moved
silently through the bushes and across the field.

From the darkness near the bridge, I stared at the cottage
silhouetted by streetlights. Delirious with anticipation, needing to get out of town, I paused but a moment. No one had
found the suitcase. Since we needed nothing in the case that
night, we simply grabbed it and headed east on the track carrying it by turns.

In town, we scrambled down a bank, which was raised for
the viaduct of the north-south track, and made our way to
bushes north of the depot. A streetlight dimly filtered
through the bushes, and we tried to relax around a black-
ened circle of stones used by hoboes. No sooner were we settled, than a distant murmur was heard above the sounds of
nighttime Owatonna.

"Must be it," Dale said, as the sound became distinct. We
left the bushes, stood beside the track, waiting. The train
rounded the bend, its glaring headlight outlining my friends.
Suddenly, its whistle moaned, grew to a banshee shriek, then
faded to a low wail. Sounding much as it had from the dorm,
only louder, terrifying. Hissing steam and rumbling were beyond anything imagined from c-16. I suddenly felt very small.

The freight slows to snatch a mail bag or something, Billy had said. I held the suitcase, a remnant, perhaps, of an earlier arrival at the school. It was heavy, bulging, but wrapped with cord, it seemed it would hold.

Suddenly bellowing, still fifty yards away, the engine spun in place, its drivers caught and it charged toward us with steady powerful throbs. Leaning out as he passed, the engineer surprised me, considering our age and the hour of night, by waving to us. Nevertheless, I aligned my eyes with his and waved back, quickly glancing aside. It was next to impossible for me to more than glance into an adult's face, especially staff—like searching for misery.

The engine disappeared into the tunnel, the powerful blasts, as it passed us, became dull chugs from the other side of the viaduct. Cars rumbled past accelerating ominously, faster than I had estimated. The wind from the train fluffed our T-shirts and tossed our hair as we leaned near to see what cars came past the depot. Half the train passed, still no open boxcars. A flatcar came past the depot. Maybe our only chance.

"Quick, Billy! The flatcar," I shouted. "The ladder on the end!"

Billy jumped, but hesitated to reach for the car only yards away. Dale, running alongside, brushed past him, grabbed the rung at the rear of the car and swung easily—as though it wasn't the first time—onto the car. He reached down and helped Billy climb on. Crawling to the center of the car, Billy lay flat.

It was hard running alongside the car holding the ladder rung, and my gait was hampered by the heavy case. In desperation, I pulled myself toward the flatcar and swung the case while thrusting hard with my grounded foot. The bottom of the case erupted. Three of everything, food, flashlight, knife and all were strewn along the tracks. My stride failed when the case emptied. With one foot on the rung, the other in space, I released the case and clung precariously as we gained speed. For a moment I thought to leap off before I fell, but Dale reached down, grabbed my belt, and rolled me onto the deck, holding me until I caught my balance. We went through the tunnel and out the other side.

9

The engine belched clouds of smoke that swirled in the blackness, choking, burning our eyes and nostrils. Cinder ash itched my scalp, worked its way under my belt and inside my т-shirt. The train accelerated, rumbled louder, its clickity-clack taunting us that we were prisoners, unable to escape. Everything became exaggerated—a nightmare—as we tunneled through the fumes of hell hurtling into the night. Billy's fear grew deeper as the miles thundered by.

Though he said little, his talk was jerky and high-pitched. When we crawled to the front edge of the flatcar, gripping the leading edge, Billy would lay nowhere but between Dale and me. If I moved away, he nervously gripped my arm, pulling me back, begging me not to leave him.

. . .

I don't know how much time had passed when Dale yelled over the rumbling, "Keep yer heads down; there's a guy on the platform!" I buried my head in my arms, but peered out at a man standing level with and one short step away from the flatcar. The man seemed too surprised to move and simply stared, pointing at us from a forward lean, blurting, "Hey you boys! What're you doing there?" The man was helpless—no small revelation to me—as State School boys rode by, right under his nose. The man's arm sagged as we rumbled off. Movie images of wartime railroad guards were fresh in my mind, and I was certain the phones would be busy, and we would be taken off when the train stopped—wherever.

I wished a thousand times for the night to end. With clenched teeth I peered once down into the blackness between cars where my darkest thoughts seethed amid the clatter and the rush of air. *It'd be easy to fall or even jump off—to die instantly. That boy at c-15 who fell through glass. Did he just give up and jump?*

The rumbling and swaying numbed me, but it was dangerous to sleep. For much of the night I curled my arms around my head; whenever I felt myself drifting, I lifted my head and looked around for a sign that our ordeal might end, anything to cling to. Then, finally, the first glow of dawn tinged the horizon and I could begin to make out our surroundings. "Dawn's here!" I yelled, which sounded more like a crow cawing. Dale and Billy raised their heads and together we watched the countryside emerge, first in silhouette, then with depth and color.

The train stopped at a small town. We slid tiredly off the flat car, found an empty boxcar on the opposite side of the train and climbed in. With time only to adjust myself to sitting, our car was banged hard, rolling me onto my back where I remained, almost instantly draining into a deep sleep, unaware of rumbling and whistle blasts.

Weather data: St. Paul, July 31, 1943: 94 degrees, 78 percent humidity under clear skies.

Later, without fully awakening us, our car was sidetracked at a small town south of St. Paul. It was quiet when I awoke dripping sweat near midday. *A scorcher*, Cory would have called it. I remember thinking, *It's dinnertime at the school.* Dale and Billy stood in the doorway and, seeing me awake, pointed at a boy who walked along the street that crossed the track.

"Ask him about water and food?" Billy asked.

"Be all right, I guess," I said. Dale and Billy stepped to the ground and sauntered toward the boy who seemed ready to run, but stood a safe distance as my friends questioned him. Back in the boxcar, Dale nodded toward the boy who had turned and headed back into town glancing once over his shoulder at us.

"No trains on weekends," Dale said. "Water up the street, though." We were very hungry, but needed water most. We located the well, drank to nearly bloating, as though we drank to satisfy our hunger too. We rested on a bench near the fountain and argued what next to do. It seemed risky being around people, which had been our downfall in Waseca, and, with options limited by our naïveté, we decided to walk the rails.

The railroad right-of-way became an oven in the brilliant, unrelenting sun. Not one wisp of cloud marked the sky, even the occasional breezes were stifling, and the extreme humidity sent sweat running off us. Leaves hung motionless from trees along the track. The tree line was shimmering illusions dancing with heat in the distance. I can't say why we didn't see heat, thirst, and hunger as adversaries before we struck off. I just wanted more distance between the school and us.

We dragged along, Dale and I falling back by turns to be with Billy who lagged constantly. A nod of the head, a finger twitch, or subtle arm movement was talk enough when each knew what needed doing. The track was an endless ribbon, the town never quite disappearing behind us, but when I looked back once, suddenly it was gone. Everything moved in slow motion, appearing, becoming familiar then tiresome, before fading slowly behind.

The sun had moved just west of high noon when we stopped at a gravel road crossing the track. We stared at a farm on its dead end.

"They might give water," Dale said.

"Maybe food," Billy added.

"Nobody gives food," Dale said.

I shrugged in resignation, pointing at the farmhouse. "We hafta ask for water anyhow. Don't we?"

"Sure, why not?" Dale said.

"Cause we'll die if we don't," I snapped.

"You don't have to get huffy," Dale said. He headed toward the farm, with Billy and me behind.

A woman stepped out of the house as we wandered into the farmyard. Middle-aged, she wore a wrinkled apron over a print dress, her hair was in a bun and her glasses sat low on her nose. She looked like a younger Miss Monson or that strict teacher whose name I can't recall.

"Good afternoon, boys," the woman said with unmistakable chill.

Dale and I looked bashfully at the ground.

"Can we have some water?" Billy asked, his fingers nervously twined together, and the corners of his mouth sagged like his shoulders. He looked worse than unhappy, but was best at talking to outsiders.

The woman carefully watched us and, without uncrossing her arms, she pointed with one finger toward a tin cup hanging on the pump. "Help yourself," she said, her voice crisp, cautious.

We drank ourselves full again then thanked her almost in unison.

As Dale and I turned toward the road, Billy paused and shyly stepped toward her, asking, "Do you have bread and ja—?"

"You boys have a good day, now," the woman interrupted, her tone flat. Her arms still crossed, she waved us off with one palm, after which she turned toward the house.

Billy stepped back, snapping his head to gaze blankly at Dale as if he had been slapped hard. The rebuff was expected, but I wanted to scream as I watched her disappear behind the screen door. Trudging back toward the tracks, I looked back once to see a curtain pulled aside and a figure looking out.

The heat was unbearable as we started down the rails, my mouth again becoming parched. I weakened faster than before and moved slowly after sitting for a time to avoid the dizziness with blurred vision and dancing spots. And that distant shimmering, was it just heat waves?

Billy collapsed near a swamp. Dale and I, too young and fatigued to realize the seriousness of his weakness—or our own—doused him and ourselves with brackish water until he improved. After resting, Billy agreed to keep moving.

Farther on, we spotted a cement stock tank nestled in a shady pasture. Artesian water, sparkling as it flowed from a pipe, lured us to drink and rest, then drink again. We rested a very long time, and I imagined sleeping forever in that shady haven, but I knew we couldn't.

"We got to keep going or we just ain't going to make it," I said.

Dale muttered, "Unless we plan to die here."

I felt better, though still listless, as we climbed the grade and started down the track. Dale and I slowly walked beside Billy.

We had all but outgrown old t-shirts, the sleeves shrunk nearly to the shoulders and the lower hem pulled up from our waists. By late afternoon, before realizing it, we were all severely sunburned. Dale's blistered bright cherry, Billy turned almost maroon, and I was a deep auburn. Not realizing our sunburns would more than sting, we plodded on in the intense sunshine.

The track aggregate burned our feet, forcing us to walk the cooler north grade, which caused my troublesome knee to ache. We all complained of sore ankles, walking there just long enough to cool our tennis shoes, which were all but falling off by now. We found twine to wrap our shoes, extending their usefulness for a while. Soon, a large opening appeared to our right, which sloped down to a lake.

"Mississippi River widens and goes kinda slow," Billy murmured, almost to himself. The obvious needed no debate and we shuffled down to the water.

My sunburn stung sharply as water touched it, but I eased into the water, clothes and all, squatting to immerse completely. We all undressed while soaking, and rinsed our clothes. Then, driven by that eternal thirst, I let water run into my mouth and swallowed. I can't say whether Dale or Billy drank. Having eaten nothing since supper the previous day and with little energy to warm us, we soon cooled to almost shivering and crawled out on hands and knees. We hung our clothes on bushes to dry then stretched out and slept.

I awoke in deeper shade to see Dale awake. He had donned his pants and, without a T-shirt, appeared haggard with a white chest and sunburn blisters on his arms, neck, and face. Billy looked the least gaunt though his sunburn was beginning to blister too. Pants and T-shirts on, belts buckled loosely in the last holes, we continued north. Our struggle must have taken us over ten miles by evening. We walked in welcome shade, but my sunburn felt as though the sun still scorched.

Stopping beneath a concrete bridge over the tracks, we climbed high on the bank beneath it where we each found a level spot and lay down. Billy slept almost instantly while Dale and I whispered. I was exhausted but ached terribly, and my sunburn kept me from sleeping other than on my back. To keep my arms from rubbing the ground, I tied my wrists with twine to my belt in front.

In the morning, numb and weak, I stared at the concrete underside of the bridge. One arm remained fastened, but the sunburn felt no worse on the other. Unwilling to move, I faced my head east and stared at the track below until the first rays of sunshine glinted on the rails.

Dale sat on one foot and leaned forward, his temple resting on the other leg while he stared at the brightening world. Still sleeping, Billy seemed more at peace than the day before. Sleep smoothed his forehead, and the anxiety-purse of his mouth was gone, but he still looked awful. He soon groaned and sat bleary eyed, his forehead wrinkling again. The tip of his tongue squeezed through tight lips and he gazed at me, misery creeping into his eyes.

"Used to hate hash, now I'd eat three helpings," Dale said, steadying himself against the bridge. Little more was said as we descended to the track and straggled north, no longer searching for anything but water.

High, scattered clouds streaked the west, but clear skies threatened another day of searing heat. No one spoke more than necessary through the morning, and we spent long periods sitting on the track breathing heavily.

We slept in a shady pasture near midday, mostly in cat naps, too tired and achy for sound sleep. Each time I awoke, I felt less like pushing on. Clouds formed while we rested, but the temperature remained in the nineties. Their shade above the railroad grade made it feel tolerably cooler, easing our trek as we pushed the rest of the afternoon toward the city.

The city had seemed elusive during two days of walking but, suddenly, we were in South St. Paul, then downtown St. Paul. We found shelter near the river under a concrete roadway, the earthwork of which sloped down to the railroad tracks. Hunger continued to gnaw at us again, and with time left before sunset, we decide to climb up the hill looking for food.

Billy seemed to have built a wall between himself and us. His trip was already done; he needed only circumstance through which to exit. A small green with a fountain and benches was near the rim of the hill, where we drank, then flopped on the grass. Sighing endlessly, I thought how easy it would be to stop breathing.

Billy stood and pointed at an alley across the street.

"Got to pee," he mumbled, gazing along his arm as he talked.

There was something strange in his voice and manner, but too exhausted to figure it out, Dale and I waved him on. Billy went down the alley without once looking back and disappeared behind buildings. After some time, Dale and I decided that he must have turned himself in. We were somber as we returned to our nest under the overpass.

There had been no weekend trains from Owatonna to the Twin Cities. In the wee hours after midnight, a monster thundered below us. Smoke and cinders billowed up, collecting under the overpass, nearly smothering us before we rolled down beside the rumbling boxcars. It was still dark after the train passed so we climbed back up to sleep longer.

We awoke at dawn and followed the track around a jutting of the hill.

"Wow," Dale whispered, as a railroad yard appeared. "Whole trains, looks like." Hoping to find a boxcar with food, we shuffled furtively across an open space to the greatest concentration of cars. I felt vulnerable in full view of railroad men seen at the far end of the yard.

"What would happen if someone caught us here?" I asked.

"Dunno," Dale said. "Better be careful though, the railroad cops have gats."

"Guns?" I said, my voice sounding more like a whisper. "They wouldn't use them on us, would they?"

"Dincha hear about those two guys who ran away couple years ago?" Dale said. "Talk is they was gunned down in Mankato."

I caught the tired glint in Dale's eyes.

"Dontcha know," I grumbled, "it's bad luck wrong to tell stories right when it could happen?"

After strolling about the yard, we were convinced the boxcars contained only steel, lumber, or were empty. A man from the other side of the yard saw us and started our way.

"Looks like we're headed back to the State School," I said.

"Follow me," Dale said. He walked away from the railroad car, but we were forced to walk near the man.

"Hello, boys," the man said. "Better not let the super catch you out here."

We were surprised that the man did not try to catch us, and we sat to plan our next move.

"Hey," Dale said and pointed under a boxcar. Following his

finger I saw water drip from a car one row over. "Refrigerator," I whispered. We shuffled to the next row.

The refrigerator cars had insulated double doors that swung outward, which were easier to open than the sliding doors of boxcars. Dale found a scrap-iron rod, broke the seal, and we desperately pried at the door. My hands trembled with the prospect of finding food and the dread of an empty car. The door creaked open.

"Holy Cow," I said softly.

Crates of fresh fruit were stacked to the ceiling. Our eyes opened wider then they had in days. Adrenaline flowed through us, and we burned the last of our energy tearing crates apart. With closed eyes, I ate handfuls of pears and apricots. Juice ran from the corners of our mouths and fruit pits dribbled near our feet. We had eaten our fill and, at mid-day, it was no longer hot as Dale and I sat with four crates of fruit in the corner of a boxcar. Planning to stay awake to watch for railroad workers, I don't remember when I slipped into a deep stupor.

Jarred awake by a giant sledgehammer, I awoke huddled to myself. My first clear awareness was of boxcar wheels squealing on curving yard rails. Listless after what seemed a very long sleep, I crawled on hands and knees to the door where Dale already sat, and peered through soiled locks ruffling over my face.

"Wonder what time it is?" he said.

"Before dawn," I said, sighing tiredly.

"Maybe it's night again. We coulda slept a whole day, you know."

"If you say so," I muttered.

It puzzled me how we fell asleep in a boxcar headed north.

We sat in the doorway, legs dangling out, watching city lights while eating fruit, my first midnight snack. With food and rest, we discussed things too sensitive for thirsty, sunburned minds.

"The watchman wouldn't check beds at c-16, would he?" I asked into the dimness. "Leastways, I never saw him."

"Nah, the assistants do that," Dale replied. "He just woke bed wetters. Took them to the pot an' that."

"Pee your bed?" I asked.

"What's it to ya," Dale said. We could see each other, but in little detail. I frowned peering into the dark haze outside. The train wound slowly through the city into the countryside. It was a gentle ride, free of cinder ash and smoke. Rail clicks and the steady laboring of the engine were assurances that our quest was not over. Soon, the glitter of city lights faded in the distance.

We had been awake and on our way less than an hour before dawn brightened the horizon. Our door faced west. The countryside emerged, first in shades of black and white, then in color as the gold sunrise lit the tops of wooded knobs. The sun was still yellow when the train slowed to a wheezing stop at a small town. We scanned the village for green apples, grapes, or anything to supplement our stores of fruit.

"Looks to be a big garden over there," I said, pointing. "What do you think'd happen if they caught us?"

"Dunno," Dale drawled. A hay stem seemed to sag off his lips. "Just run like hell."

"Can't outrun bullets," I said. "Right now, I couldn't even outrun Fatso."

But I was too hungry to be cautious. We left the boxcar and headed into the village where a side lane led to the large garden. With my t-shirt tied into a sack, we dug up and snapped off a variety of vegetables. It was early enough for the owner to be in bed and, though we were not chased, we were hastened by fear.

On the way to the train, Dale found a two-quart bottle. He took it to the depot for water while I, sack in hand, went to the boxcar. I approached the train from behind a tree surrounded by low bushes. I remained hidden while eyeing a trainman who leaned against our boxcar.

I stepped forward for a better look, when my foot caught on a root. I fell out in full view of the man, my t-shirt sack falling without spilling beside me. The man spun around and started toward me. Recovering, I sat, leaning forward, fiddling with frayed shoelaces and pretended not to notice him. I had learned at the State School not to acknowledge approaching staff until they spoke.

"You okay, boy?" the man said. He didn't sound mean. "Injun, huh?"

I looked up. He was big, wore bib overalls, like Mr. Kruger, and held a wrench in a large hand. Standing, I nervously faced the man and slowly lifted the sack to my shoulder.

The man seemed surprised, "Sure you're all right, boy?" he asked.

Without thinking, I stepped back staring at the wrench.

He stopped. "I'm not going to hurt you," he said.

I realized suddenly how terrible I must have looked, the same as Dale appeared to me. Scrawny, filthy, and sunburned, we could be suffering terminal something-or-other.

"I'm fine," I said hoarsely. "Just stopped to rest." I shifted the sack for emphasis. "Getting heavy, better get home."

"You don't look good," the man persisted. He sounded sincere, but I remained wary. I thought he might be trying to get close enough to grab me, but the man made no sudden movement, so I turned toward the bushes. That seemed to satisfy him. I heard him slowly, then in a normal pace, head on toward the caboose.

Dale approached, I waved him toward my bush, and we both watched through parted bushes as the man went inside the caboose. With no more signs of railroad workers, we went to the boxcar, settling down just as the sun rose above the trees. Scraping new carrots with a tin we ate raw vegetables with the greatest relish ever. At the school, we were forced to eat vegetables, which was usually all right, but I despised fried green tomatoes, fried egg plant and raw onion. Now, the weather was just right, our boxcar was comfortable, and our burgeoning larder made me feel like we were doing all right.

It was comfortable, riding inside as the train continued north, but the hours dragged. To pass the time, we tossed things at telephone poles and tried to joke. By late afternoon, the sun no longer warmed. It would be a cold, miserable night. Hunching over crossed arms, we stared at the passing countryside and talked little. The train slowed on its approach to a small collection of buildings on an up-slope west of the tracks. *Not much of a town*, I thought. The train bumped softly to a stop.

Gazing out as the engine softly chugged again, we watched the ground move the other way. We were being sidetracked. It concerned me that our boxcar would be disconnected as it had been south of St Paul, but the engine wheezed and vented comfortably and I knew we would sit a while.

I scanned out at the village and backed in. "A man just went around the front of the engine," I said. "Looks clear now, though. Wonder how long to sunset." I shivered the words into fragments and hugged myself with goose-bumped arms. They were still too sore to rub warm.

"Not long now," Dale said. "Half hour, maybe." He took the water bottle, peered out, then stepped down. "Let's go," he said, heading toward the village. I stepped down, squinted up and down the track, and followed him.

No one was out as we walked up the main street. A community hand pump on a village green seemed our only source of water. Two boys of high school age appeared from an alley across the street and paused to stare. We ignored them and I began pumping. The handle worked loosely and dry scraping was heard from deep in the bowels of the pump, but no water came.

"Must be dry," I muttered, giving the handle a shake.

Dale tried pumping, but to no avail and stood silent behind me. He suddenly gripped my shoulder and pointed toward the boys across the street. "They're comin' after us, looks like," he said.

Thinking they might be only curious, we let the boys approach, but when they were close enough, each grabbed one of us.

I cried out. The taller one seemed surprised. "I'm just holding your arms," he said.

"I'm sunburned. Can't you see?" I squawked.

"Yeah, we didn't do nothing," Dale said. He seemed ready to fight, but contained himself.

"Hey, yer Indian," the tall boy exclaimed.

"So?" I replied.

"Didn't think Injuns got sunburned," the boy said. "Yer both dirty hoboes, looks like to me." He looked hard at me, then at Dale.

"Gypsies came through here last year. You're not them coming back?"

The shorter boy let go of Dale. "Injuns don't run with Gypsies," he said. "They're on their own, all right."

"You gonna call the cops or let us go?" Dale asked, squaring off to the boys. "We're looking for work and stopped for water."

The tall boy murmured thoughtfully, "That'd be your freight then." He nodded toward the tracks.

"Yeah," I said.

The boy holding my arms released me. "How come an Indian and a white boy are running together?" he asked.

As I shrugged in response, a train whistled far to the north.

"Here, I'll help you get water," the taller one interrupted. "Better hurry, the freight takes off soon's the passenger train is gone."

"We tried getting water, but the pump's broken or something," Dale said.

The tall boy grinned, pointing to a pail of water near the pump. "It's called priming. You gotta pour water in the top and pump quick until the water comes. Then pump until the water looks clear. You could get sick if you drink bad water."

The boys watched as we filled the bottle, then waved us off. "Good luck," the taller boy called after us.

"Thanks for the help," Dale called back. I nodded.

Soon, we stood in the door of our boxcar looking out. The sleek diesel passenger train rounded the bend north of town and passed us only yards away.

Twilight faded as our train chugged north and the countryside dimmed to now familiar blacks and grays. In less than half an hour the train stopped at another small town. It wasn't clear why the train stopped, but boot steps soon approached and stopped one car down. We pressed into a corner on the door side of our car as the boot steps were again heard, closer. They stopped outside our doorway and the dim outline of a man's head and shoulders leaned in the doorway. The man disappeared from view, and I shivered as the door slammed shut encasing us in blackness.

Soon, the engine chugged and our car lurched into motion. We tried to open the door, but could not coordinate efforts in the dark. After much pushing and prying, we abandoned our efforts and went to sleep.

I couldn't help thinking we might die from the cold. The constant rumble and the engineer's mournful warning for highway crossings became a constant reminder that we were trapped with no escape.

At dawn a sliver of light glimmering about the door stirred us awake. Using the wood ends from the fruit crates, we pried and pushed until we cracked the door enough so both of us could get a hand on it. In spite of fatigue, we forced it open, then sat in the open doorway taking in the sun-flooded landscape. The sun soon warmed the car and once more we fell into a deep sleep of exhaustion.

A whistle screamed, waking us. After kneeling and staring numbly at the passing landscape, I realized it was late afternoon. Dale breathed more deeply after resting, though his blistered face still looked terrible. The train slowed to a horse trot. He roused, moaned quietly, then crawled on hands and knees to the door. He stood against the frame, leaning out.

"Hey, there's a bridge up ahead," he said. "Gotta go."

He leaned on the vertical frame of the doorway and faced out.

"Better watch it or you'll really be Chief Rain in the Face."

"Flush the pot, I gotta go, too," I said.

Dale gave me a painful sunburned smile.

The engine rounded a sweeping bend and squared off on its approach to the bridge, a fragile structure with no guard rails and long, spindly poles supporting a narrow track bed. I worried that a train—our train—would be too heavy for such a structure. But our car passed the center of the span with no thundering collapse, and the scene from an open boxcar became a beautiful panorama of forested hills and valleys. The stuff of slide shows at the State School auditorium.

By late afternoon, feeling numb, I felt helpless to face more problems. Though I had planned to leave the boxcar and make my way to the reservation, I had lost my nerve. I couldn't leave our home until it quit taking us where it was going.

The air was crisp as our train entered the outskirts of a larger town at dusk.

"Superior," Dale mumbled as we passed the yard sign. He sounded dejected.

"Superior is in Wisconsin," I said, "I've never been here. Think there's a place for a person to go for the night and leave in the morning?"

"A movie showed the Salvation Army givin' people food an' a place to sleep," Dale said.

"That'd be salvation, all right," I said. "They have to sing hymns first, don't they?"

"Yeah," Dale agreed.

The train rumbled slowly into town and after backing up, stopped in a railroad yard alongside other strings of cars. The sky had turned black, like it would on a cold, moonless night in February. We stepped into a world of tracks and twinkling stars, walking stiffly between rows of boxcars. The diffusion of city lights dimly outlined boxcars. Reaching into open cars, I felt the floor around the doorway. I reached inside one car and palmed along the floor.

"Hold it," I said. "Paper insulates, right? There's long sheets of it here."

Stiff, smooth paper stretched as far as I could reach.

"It's heavy and maybe two layers thick, I think."

I climbed into the car and, on all fours, explored the extent of the paper. One at a time, we held one end of a sheet of paper, rolled over and over wrapping ourselves in layers of paper—a cocoon. We slid out, retrieved the remaining fruits and vegetables, then climbed into our paper tubes to escape a deepening chill. Faces to the air, we crumpled the paper about our shoulders to hold in the heat. I fell hard asleep.

"Come out of there!"

The voice jarred me awake.

"Come out! We know you're in there!"

The words were loud and sharp. I shoved my head into the cold and blinked into strong lanterns flooding the car. I peered at Dale, propped on elbows, who also squinted into the light. I don't know whether the men stalked or accidentally found us. Two figures leaned in the door. It sounded like more were nearby. I held my hands out to shield against the blinding lights.

"Snap it up!" someone barked.

Two hands grabbed for my wrists. I flinched my arms up, tried to sidestep, but the hands flew down and grabbed my ankles. As I fell out the door, I was caught by others and set on the ground gently enough, but one man would not release his painful grip on my upper arms.

"My arms are sunburned," I said. The man shone his light on my arm, then grabbed my wrists which were the least burned.

"We didn't do anything wrong, let us go, and we'll leave your railroad," I said.

"Kids yer age can't run loose. Ain't healthy."

With our odyssey ended, I sobbed, quiet at first, then uncontrollably, harder than anytime in years. It was embarrassing, crying so hard in front of the men and Dale, but I couldn't stop. I looked up through watery eyes at Dale who also sobbed. We had never seen each other cry. The men did not talk while we cried, but held our wrists so we couldn't wipe our eyes. They were gentler after we sobered.

"Hey, we got an Indian here," one man said. I glanced up at him.

"Those are bad sunburns," another said.

"How long you been gone from home?" the man holding

my right arm asked. "Can't talk, huh?" He reached toward me. I flinched sideways and banged my head against the car.

I winced and bent away from the man.

"You all right?" the man asked, talking softly. "Pretty touchy. Let me look at your head."

The man took a step nearer.

"Only a scratch and bump. It'll be all right," he said.

A police car arrived at the end of the yard, two men got out and approached down the aisle. Held behind the men, up to then, I was suddenly jerked into the glare of an officer's flashlight.

"This one's Injun," one proudly stated. "Seems both are from the same place. Good thing we found them, poor kids."

"Going to get real cold tonight," another man said.

"What did they do?" the officer asked.

"Sleeping in the boxcar," a man said.

"Is that all? If we put everyone in jail that slept in a boxcar, we'd have the jails full."

He pointed at the man holding me.

"Do you need to hold them? They don't look dangerous. I'm sure county social services will know what to do. Looks like they'll need clothing and a bath and something for those. . . ." He peered closer at Dale, "Looks like, sunburns. I'll have to report to the sergeant first." He motioned us toward his car. "You look cold. Better jump in the car and warm up."

We limped to the car. We told the officer our names and about the State School on our way to the jail. I knew it was over.

Near midnight we stood awkwardly between the two officers before a high desk. The intake officer, called from home to officiate, appeared surprised and leaned over his desk staring down at us.

"What's the charge?" he asked, louder than necessary.

The kind officer from the railyard looked at us, then to his companion, "I . . . I'm not sure," he said, shrugging, "Would it be running away?"

"We have no facilities for runaways at this jail," the intake officer boomed. He lowered his pen and stared at us.

"Put them in the back cell with double bunks until Owatonna sends for them."

The kind officer acted surprised.

"Lock them up? They haven't done anything."

Flushing with poorly controlled anger, the intake officer leaned over his desk, his pen pointed at us.

"We can't have juveniles running loose around town now, can we? Lock 'em up!"

"They need a bath, clean clothes. . . . And those burns," the officer persisted. "With no charge, shouldn't we call social welf—"

"They look all right to me, lock 'em up!" He entered our non-arrest in the blotter. "The cell on the end."

The jailer, apparently called in to work as well, herded us to the end cell of the empty three-cell jail. Dale faced him as we passed him.

"Kin we have somethin' to eat?"

The jailer locked the door, paused, and stared through the bars.

"Breakfast is in the morning."

Though it was our first night inside a building since leaving Owatonna, it was cold in the jail and the jailer departed before we realized the bunks had no blankets.

"Hey, anybody there?" Dale yelled into the corridor. "We got no blankets, and the window's broke. Hey, it's cold in here." Only silence, no sounds of life anywhere in the jail.

10

Miss Monson loathed me. She hated my sullen si-lence, my quiet disrespect. To punish me, when I was barely ten years old, she made me sit for hours in a cramped mop closet. I was concealed there, knees tight to my chest. I would wrap my arms around my legs, or sit on my hands, when the cement floor was cold, to keep my rump warm. I have no memory of why, but I sat entire evenings there, beginning soon after supper, listening to the sounds of play through

*the vents low in the door. Sometimes I dozed, head
on knees. After the other boys went to bed, I sat in
eerie quiet. Just before she was ready to go to sleep,
Miss Monson would pull the door open.*

*"Get to bed," she'd say. "Next time you'll behave,
won't you?" It was painful, after hours of squatting,
to stand quickly, but to avoid a shove or a whack,
I shuffled hastily, stiffly, to bed.*

. . .

We were the sole occupants of a three-cell jail. When the jailer
left, one hall light remained on, and the jail grew tomb-quiet.

"Everyone's gone for the night," Dale said.

"Probably. There'll be nothing doing 'til morning, then,"
I said.

"If the place burns down, we're goners," Dale grumbled.

"Wouldn't mind the heat," I said, smirking.

That night was a struggle to survive the cold. Dale took the
thin mattress off the top bunk, and laid it on the bottom mattress. We then squeezed between mattresses, against each
other. We mumbled about returning to the school until sleep
quieted us.

"Breakfast." It was a different jailer, and he clanged the
bars noisily, rudely, with his key ring.

I opened my eyes to see him staring straight at me, his face
pressed against the bars. He held two cups and a paper plate.
The jailer's obesity was exaggerated by a short wide frame,
and he had a dull look to his face.

"Come on, I ain't got all day. If you don't want it, I'll go," he
growled.

I sniffed, but our breakfast had no odor. Dale took a cold sandwich, which contained one slice of bologna smeared with a white spread. The jailer then handed him a cup of warm brown drink.

"This all we get?" Dale said.

"Lucky you get that. Give it back if you don't want it."

"We can do better on our own," Dale said. The jailer looked at me but did not offer the sandwich. I poked Dale from behind—however meager, it was our first meat and bread in a week.

"Here, Chief," the jailer said.

I took the sandwich, ate ravenously, and drank the awful coffee, simply because it was warm. Dale and I talked briefly after eating, then slept on individual bunks until awakened later by the same man rattling his keys on the bars. He seemed to enjoy harassing us.

"Dinner time, come and get it," he said in a sarcastic singsong.

Dale went quickly to the door, grabbed a sandwich and cup. Stepping back, he waved the sandwich over his head. "Food's a fancy name fer this thing," he said.

"Don't get smart with me!" the jailer snarled.

"We didn't ask to be here," Dale said.

"Nobody does."

"Well, we did nothing wrong," Dale said. "Running away from that hell can't be illegal. And how come we got no blankets? It's cold in here." He slurped, spilling some of his drink on the floor. I extended my hand for the sandwich, which the jailer did not offer. Instead he glared at me, and I pulled my hand back.

"What you got to say, Injun?" he sneered, but he gruffly shoved the sandwich through the bars. "Here."

A more civil jailer brought supper, after which Dale and I talked until we grew sleepy.

Almost immediately, it seemed, it was morning and we were awakened by the obese jailer. "Yer breakfast," he said. Our diet never varied. Sleeping against the wall, I kneed Dale, who rolled out and reached for a sandwich. I took my sandwich, and we ate sitting on the bunk.

The jailer did not leave and continued to stare at us. He coughed and his midsection jumped. I looked at Dale who had also stopped eating and we both stared.

"What you looking at?" the jailer said. He sounded piqued—childishly piqued.

"Nothin'," Dale replied, calmly biting his sandwich.

"Yer leaving today," the jailer said.

Dale and I sat up looking at each other. "When?" I asked.

"Now," the jailer said as he unlocked the door. He suddenly stared hard at me. "Hey, the Injun can talk English."

"You can eat on the run," he said.

Dale dumped his drink in the basin as he started toward the open door. "What was that junk anyway?"

The jailer faced me, "You don't like our food, neither, I suppose?" he growled. "Git, before I change my mind." Following Dale, I pulled my head low to my shoulders, as I passed the jailer.

Halfway down the corridor, Dale looked around at me. "A week in here, and we'd starve to death," he said.

I laughed to myself. "Forsooth, twas the hemlock and nigh to do us in," I said. The heavy steps behind quickened and I was shoved hard in the back. Still limping and without energy to resist, I stumbled awkwardly into the main room where I caught myself against a chair. That might have grown nastier were not others present in the intake room. Though no one had checked on us in the jail, a small crowd gathered to witness our departure.

"We're getting rid of them," came a whisper from my right.

No sooner had I straightened from the shove, than I saw the social worker. I knew him by his surprise. He had been walking in our direction when I burst into the room. Now he was stopped dead in a forward lean.

Straightening, the social worker shot a disdainful look to the obese head jailer, then looked back to us, drawing a deep breath. "You're Peter, and you must be Dale," he said, scrutinizing us. Our necks, arms, and faces were smudged with dirt, our hair matted, and we wore filthy ragged clothes and disintegrating sneakers. The social worker looked back to the head jailer.

"I take it the jail has no bathing facilities," he began. "Were they examined for illness? Anything can happen to youngsters in a week." He leaned close to inspect my head bruise. "It's fresh enough. I'd hate to guess how *that* happened!"

Dale pointed at my head, "Well, when the railroad men caught us, they—"

"I was not aware of any bruise," the head jailer interrupted. "Not in the jail, were they hurt."

"Then, it's obvious you didn't check them," the social worker continued. "They look to be suffering from exposure, and those filthy clothes could aggravate sunburn and body sores. By their looks, you didn't feed them."

The head jailer coughed nervously with one finger on his jaw. "It was them that ran away," he said. "The city says we're to hold homeless juveniles . . . for their own good."

"For their good, you say?" The social worker spoke softly, but his voice ran with contempt. "I certainly wouldn't want you doing anything for *my* good."

The social worker drove us to the train depot and introduced us to the conductor. "This man will see to you to the Cities. Mr. Doleman, perhaps you know him, will pick you up there. Good luck," he said as he turned to go.

The conductor motioned at a seat near the front of the car.

"Both of you sit together and don't move. Ask if you need the toilet," he said. He was gentle enough but seemed preoccupied.

When the couple in the seat ahead of us held their tickets up for the conductor to see, the woman asked, "Where are they going?"

The conductor leaned toward the couple and murmured from the side of his mouth, "They're runaways going back to an orphanage." The conductor moved on, and the couple whispered between themselves. They turned in their seat and faced us with genuine smiles, but their sympathy made me even more embarrassed.

"You boys look starved," the woman said, handing us each a bread roll.

"Something to hold you over 'til you get wherever you're going," the man said. His voice faltered as though unsure of whether he should help us, but he handed us each fifty cents.

The couple faced forward and did not turn around for the remainder of the trip.

Our return on the passenger car took half as many hours as it took days walking and riding in boxcars. We passed back over the trestle and through that little town where the older boys stopped us and by the vegetable garden. Was it all only a dream?

The train slowed, quietly stopping at a Twin Cities station.

"Don't move, boys," the conductor said, touching Dale's shoulder. "Until we see Mr. Doleman." After the last passenger was gone, he scanned the platform through the windows of our car.

"There he is," Dale said. He leaned across the aisle and pointed to a man on the platform who watched as passengers stepped from the train.

"Mr. Doleman?" the conductor called from the door. Mr. Doleman straightened, put on a smile, and approached. The conductor joined him outside, then Mr. Doleman turned and leaned in.

"Come with me, boys," he said. He spoke softly and showed no amazement. He led us to his car.

"Did you have a good trip?" Mr. Doleman asked as we drove south out of the Cities toward Owatonna. "Do you know how much gas it takes to chase after runaways? Tires are rationed for the State School, too, you know." Mr. Doleman said nothing about our appearance, nor did he ask how we felt or why we ran away—he was just doing his job.

It felt odd as I entered the campus past cottages with boys and girls playing or walking about—this was my home, though not really that. Some time soon, I knew, I would leave and never return.

Mr. Doleman took us to C-16 and turned us over to Mrs. Steele. He warned us not to consider running away again, then left. Mrs. Steele scanned us from head to foot, frowning.

"You'll certainly come to nothing when you're grown. I can't imagine idlers wanting to run away in the first place. And starving by the looks of it. Well, it's to the shower first, and Miss Klein will have clean clothes for you."

She ended with a sigh.

"Supper in an hour."

Though I was eager to shower and don clean clothes, I was most excited by the prospect of my first hot food in eight days.

I lathered and washed the grime off. It took four shampoos combined with vigorous combing to smooth my matted hair—like digging burrs from a dog's fur. Rinsing my hair for the last time, I smirked as footsteps approached.

"Now, Cole, wash behind your ears," I said, nodding at the shower door.

Dale smiled and nudged me, "Yeah." We both had our backs to the door when it flew open.

"Soap your hair good. Get rid of the animals you picked up," Miss Klein said. "And wash behind your ears." She leaned in just short of shower spray. "By the looks of things you need steel wool." I stepped out of the spray and lathered to hide behind soap suds.

"You've slimmed some in your travels, Peter," Miss Klein said.

"Since when do we need help washing?" I said.

"I'm supposed to see if you have sores and that you wash properly," Miss Klein murmured.

"Well, you seen, can we wash in privacy, now?" I said.

Miss Klein ignored us, "Your skin looks awful where it's peeling, Dale. See me after you're dry and I'll give you something for it. Wouldn't hurt to put balm on yours too, Peter. Don't take too long in there. I don't think you want to miss supper."

We talked quietly while eating our supper of hash, vegetables, milk, bread and butter, and pudding. Though hash disgusted me in the past, I thought I would eat five servings, but was stuffed after two plus pudding.

Dale and I were not given much work; our punishment was mostly on paper, and I was soon able to do the same as others.

Although maturing years in only days, I had failed to free myself from an institution. But I learned important lessons: adults outside the State School were just as miserable, kind, or indifferent as State School employees. So I accepted my lot at the State School. Though I did not have to work for Mr. Beaty anymore, I no longer feared the possibility that I might— I'd give him his cold eye back and dare him to do anything.

During my remaining year at C-16, I cleaned the gym and pool at intervals, worked in the cow barn and cleaned the operating room after surgery. I was left alone during much of my work. Then, in early June, just after Saturday breakfast, Roy and I met Mrs. Cory waiting in the hall commons of C-16. Mrs. Cory held her arm out to me and motioned Roy on. Her face was soft, and her employee self seemed missing.

"Peter, could I speak with you?" she asked. "In the living room, please."

"Now?" I asked.

"If you would," Mrs. Cory said. I entered the living room. Mrs. Cory sat in a rocker and motioned to an empty chair.

"Sit," she said.

I sat hunched forward, forearms on my lap, waiting.

"The office has agreed to let you stay overnight at my house," she said. She paused with clasped hands. "If you want to."

I sat up in my chair and looked nervously out the window. "I don't understand," I said.

"We'd go fishing," she said, "for bullheads. Then we'd have a fish fry later at our home and you'd sleep in a bunk bed under my son."

"I don't know anything about fishing or staying in anyone's house. Maybe your boy wouldn't like it, or your husband. Wouldn't I be in the way?" I worried there was more to this than she was saying, that I was being groomed for farm placement. Did the office ask her to see if I could be placed, or did she have a checklist from Doctor Yager? I looked at her hands then to her eyes. She seemed genuine, and I began to feel more at ease.

Mrs. Cory said, "My husband would show you how to fish."

"If you're sure I won't be in the way," I said.

"Of course not," Mrs. Cory assured me. She smiled. "He'll pick us up after dinner. Just wear what you have on."

The prospect of fishing and staying in a private home stunned me. If it really happened. Even as I sat in the back seat of the Corys' car, it felt wonderful beginning my first car ride ever in recreation.

Richard, their ten-year-old son, played catch with me in the backyard, where Mrs. Cory brought a snack, my second between meals, of sandwiches and sweet juice. At supper, Mr. Cory said grace, which lasted less than ten seconds, and was felt much deeper than the thirty to sixty seconds of silence at the cottage. Everyone talked over supper, which was unheard of at c-3 and c-15 and hushed at c-16.

After supper, Mr. Cory opened a metal box with compartments and trays and sorted through a miscellany of brightly colored lures.

"First, we get the fishing tackle ready," he said. Fishing gear was called tackle in movies, but I never questioned its terminology until holding some. Were we going to tackle the fish? I smiled to myself.

The Corys packed a lunch and we left for Clinton Falls. I stared at the passing countryside, restraining an inner excitement while listening to the talk of a real family—about relatives, weddings, and auctions.

The sun touched the horizon as we parked on the east side of the river below the falls. As if on cue when the sun dipped behind the hills, a cloud of bats emerged from an old mill building across the river. It was an eerie sight viewed for the first time against the lingering glow of sunset. Smells, the roaring falls, and water washing against the shore; the river seemed alive.

Mr. Cory talked as he handed me a pole, "I'll help with the first worm; you can do the rest yourself. Bullheads are best fished after dark."

"Why's that?" I asked. We talked loud to be heard over the noise of the falls.

"Their feeding time," Mr. Cory replied. "Maybe it's safer when animals and bigger fish can't see them."

"Maybe," I said, "like human animals too?"

"Yep," Mr. Cory said, smiling. "Only we don't need to see them."

I imitated the way Mr. Cory threw his line and positioned the bobber.

"See that?" Mr. Cory pointed to his jiggling bobber.

"Yes," I replied. "That's the fish, not the current. Right?"

"Yes sir," Mr. Cory said, just as the bobber disappeared. He jerked his pole and a wriggling fish sailed onto the bank.

"Holy cow!" I exclaimed, "Is that a bullhead?"

"Sure is," Mr. Cory said. "Now it's your turn."

"I don't think I'll ever catch a fish," I said.

Just then, Mr. Cory touched my arm. "Maybe quicker than you think. Careful now, you might have one." He pointed to my bobber. "Not yet." While I stared at my bobber, it suddenly disappeared.

"Now!" Mr. Cory said. I jerked the rod, a fish flew over my head nearly hitting Mrs. Cory who was worming her hook behind me.

I caught six fish by myself and we all caught a pailful. Long after dark we climbed into the car for the return trip. Exhausted by the excitement, I slept on the short trip into town.

The Corys taught me how to clean the fish, roll them in flour and fry them. My first late-night fish fry found me yawning and totally relaxed. I have no memory of climbing into bed, only of waking up before Richard. I lay in the bottom bunk wondering if the Corys who seemed to enjoy having me, were also helping Dr. Yager.

11

It wasn't until years later, when I was an adult and researching the records of the State School, that I realized that my experiences were not unique. The articles I read of farm indenture in the early years of the school were little different from its last years when I was there. Though most boys worked hard for little or no wages, a much smaller percentage of indentured boys were verbally abused or beaten by their guardian farmers. I found among some of the earliest archives, this report from 1898 of a social worker's conversation with a seventeen-year-old boy, who was first indentured at fifteen, and had apparently run away:

Social worker: Why did you leave?
Boy: I worked two long seasons for only one
    suit of clothes and ten cents one Fourth of
    July. I can do better on my own.

This boy was almost fifty years older than me. He may have been dead by the time I entered my indenture, repeating his unspoken sorrow, and finally running at the very same age.

. . .

In November, the Schaulses' third baby, Yvette, was born. It only seemed to heighten the tension between John and Emma. They became more irritable every day, shouting before and during meals, knotting my stomach. Breakfasts were eaten in icy silence, and I did not relax until I was on the school bus. When I returned home from school one afternoon, the weather was unusually warm. Uneasiness gripped me as I stepped from the bus, waved goodbye to Gene, and headed into the Schaulses' driveway: John's car was gone. Again.

On my way to change clothes, I heard sounds of Emma caring for little Yvette and knew John had gone alone to town. Early chores finished, I was in the house by six o'clock for supper. Emma often delayed my supper, hoping for John's return. With nothing to eat since school lunch, I was glad when Emma set a plate for me.

"I eat when John comes home," Emma said.

"Did he say when he was coming?" I asked between bites.

"Never mind, you get to chores," Emma said curtly. "If you not here, John would be home, not running to bars!"

"I know," I mumbled with a full mouth. After eating, holding my denim jacket, I stopped at the door and faced Emma, "I really want to go, you know." But Emma had already turned her back to me.

On my way out to begin milking, I snapped on the yard light. It dimly lit the barn and silo creating eerie outlines about the buildings, dancing, meshing with older shadows in my mind. That fear deepened as I milked. Whenever a car passed, I stood to look out the barn window, hoping it wouldn't slow, that it wasn't John.

After several false alarms, I saw John's car slow and turn into the yard. It stopped near the house. I watched through the window as John felt his way to the house. I stepped out of the barn and froze in the yard staring at the house. I knew Emma was going to sic him on me. She could divert his rage away from herself if John took out his anger on me. I almost felt sorry for Emma, but saw her as selfish and cowardly. Rather than standing up to John, or telling someone about his drinking and tirades, she would send him to the barn looking for me. The house door burst open, and those scorching eyes homed in on me.

I ran to hide behind the log pile, hoping he would tire and go to bed. I would have gladly finished chores alone. I reached the pile, stopped and looked around, relieved there was no sign of him. I sighed, relieved that John had not followed me.

Something moving atop the log pile caught the corner of my eye. I jumped with fear. There stood John, like the devil in silhouette, swinging a weapon.

"No!" I yelled.

It was the briefest image in slow motion: the dark shadow, my arm not quite shielding my face, and the outline of the weapon in the yard light. My head suddenly exploded in a shower of stars, and everything disappeared into blackness.

It seemed only seconds that I slept. I felt first a dull throb, then a blinding headache and creeping awareness. I tried to move, but nothing worked. This paralysis caused a deep sense of hopelessness; I was afraid I was dying. I stared at the barn, but the yard light was off and my eyes closed again.

I woke to a penetrating chill. I could only move my head now and looked down at myself: flat on my stomach, bent at the waist, as though reaching for my right foot. Everything was dark—the barn, the house. I heard the cows in the night corral. John had finished chores. I worried I would freeze to death while lying there fading in and out of consciousness. I thought back to the boy in Owatonna who died after a head injury. I tried to move, but—still paralyzed—I faded out again. In my nightmare, I was on the brink of a black, bottomless pit. Screaming and crawling toward a white brilliance above, I slid steadily downward.

Cold and shivering, I could now move my legs and arms. My left arm and ribs were painful to move, and my headache was indescribable. Between periods of rest, I slowly crawled on hands and knees to the road. I put my bruised head in the weeds, where I again slept until dawn tinged the east. The long night had ended.

As the sun touched the treetops in the Schaulses' yard, I stood and moved farther down the road, then sat again. Neither Emma nor John searched for me that night or in the morning. They slept in their bed, leaving me asleep outside.

A car approached as day brightened, and I motioned at it without standing. A man leaned out the window as it slowed.

"Need a ride, boy?" the man asked.

"Hi, are you going into town?" I said, standing carefully to keep my head from exploding.

"Say, you don't look good," the man said.

"I'd like a ride to town. If you're going that way, I mean." I began to sit again. "Otherwise, I got to sit down or something."

"Hop in," the man said.

"Schauls, you say? Name sounds familiar," the man said as we neared Caledonia. "Beat you last night, huh?"

"Everyone knows him in the bars," I said. "Beats Emma too—his wife." Though my thoughts became clearer, a freight train still thundered in my head.

The man stopped at a house. "He'll point you in the right direction," he said, nodding toward the house. "He's my family doctor." After knocking on the door, I waited until a man appeared in casual dress, then I stepped back, not sure what to say.

"Yes," the man asked, seeming both surprised and curious. As he looked me over, he opened the door wider and motioned me in. "You could have gone to the hospital, and they could have called me."

"That man dropped me off here. I can come back later," I said.

"Not at all," the doctor said. "Looks like he brought you here for good reason." He pointed to a treatment table. "Sit there and tell me about it. I'm Dr. Steins. Your name and age, please."

"Peter Razor," I said. "Seventeen. I feel better, but got a bad headache."

"I see. Tell me what happened," Dr. Steins insisted.

"All I remember is, he hit my head," I said. "Then that man gave me a ride here."

"Of course," Dr. Steins murmured, as he wrote. "Who hit you? What did he hit you with? Was it an accident or intentional?"

"Don't know," I replied. "I mean, I don't know what he hit me with, but he did it on purpose."

"I see," Dr. Steins said as he began to examine me. Satisfied that I was in no apparent danger, he motioned at an interior door. "It's well before office hours, and I must do a few things. You're stable, so just relax on the table. I'll be back shortly." He smiled and entered his living quarters.

The wall clock showed 8 A.M., eleven hours since the beating. When Dr. Steins returned fifteen minutes later, he was dressed in a white professional garment and asked me to undress so he could examine me.

"You may get dressed," he said when he was done. My head was still thundering.

He talked and wrote at his desk, while I buttoned my shirt. "When it comes to head injuries," he said, "we can't always tell right away. You have severe bruising and a contused skull. Fortunately, nothing appears fractured, and your upper arm is only sprained. It could have been caused by the fall. Damned idiot!"

Dr. Steins' outburst startled me. "I . . . I'm sorry about bothering you before hours," I said.

"Not you," he said, walking toward me with a tray full of bandages. "The s.o.b. who did this. Anyway, you're coming out of a bad concussion quite well, considering. You have symptoms of exposure, but lying outside in the cold might have helped your head."

He began wrapping my head. "These bandages will need to be replaced a couple times a day." He handed me a glass of water and two pills. "This will help your headache and control bleeding." He handed me a bottle. "Take two tonight and I'll see you tomorrow. I called Mr. Miller at county juvenile services. He'll be here shortly."

"Well, so you're Peter," Mr. Miller said. He had just entered and greeted Dr. Steins. "Looks like, what's his name, Schauls, worked you over pretty good."

"Beats his wife, too," I said.

"One thing at a time, Peter," Mr. Miller said. "We'll take care of you first, and talk about John later." He was a portly man, almost bald with a businesslike demeanor, but seemed concerned.

Dr. Steins handed Mr. Miller a paper. "He'll need rest. We normally hospitalize someone with this type of injury," he said, "especially after an extended period of unconsciousness, but he's already pulled through the worst part. It's already been over twelve hours, so if he can be quiet for a few days, I think he'll be fine."

He chuckled and put his hand on my shoulder. "And I have nothing against manure, but Peter might feel better if he could bathe and have some clean clothes. Lukewarm water only until the swelling goes down."

"Certainly," Mr. Miller said. "He looks like a strong young man. We can put him in with Mrs. Murray until we find a permanent home."

Mrs. Murray was a retired nurse with a spacious house, a large and secure place. In the bathroom I looked in the mirror and began to realize the extent of my injuries. My head was bloody and bruised from the right cheek and temple to the top of my head and swollen from the top of my head down to my jaw. I had a mark above my right ear and scrapes on my forehead and left cheek. My left arm and ribs were sore and bruised.

While I bathed, Mrs. Murray discarded all my clothes and laid out clean pajamas for me. She applied clean dressings and, after a light breakfast, showed me to my room. I lay in bed wondering what would happen to me until my headache vanished in sleep.

Mrs. Murray woke me for supper in bed and, the next morning, for breakfast in bed, talking as she fixed my head and took my vital signs.

"Did you know you slept eighteen hours? I brought you supper, but you looked so peaceful, I decided you need sleep more than food. How do you feel?"

"I feel better," I said. "The medicine's helping."

I felt uneasy wondering why I should be treated so well. The chill had left me weak, almost feverish, but my mind kept churning over the same question—*what's to happen now?*

Days passed. I listened to the radio, read newspapers with

less difficulty, and walked around the block in good second-hand clothes that Mr. Miller sent over. My headaches would take longer to subside. My right temple hurt and my vision problems persisted—like sleepwalking or groping through a thin mist.

Dressed in good secondhand clothes that Mr. Miller sent over, I walked with Mrs. Murray to Dr. Steins' office. We passed buildings that seemed to sway.

"You're doing remarkably well, Peter," Dr. Steins said, then turned to Mrs. Murray. "His responses are slow, but he can return to school tomorrow." As we left, Mrs. Murray told me that Mr. Miller had picked another farm family for me. In spite of concern about moving to a new farm, I felt there were no other options and agreed.

The next day I walked the short distance to the high school, wondering what the other students would say.

It seemed everyone knew everything that transpired in or out of town.

Students and teachers alike were accustomed to me being unwashed and dressed in shabby clothes. Suddenly, I was well-dressed with a clean look. My head injury was scabbed over, and my hair was neatly combed. *A freshly scrubbed look*, a teacher said with a smile. My first day of school away from the Schaulses meant getting reacquainted with classmates who seemed surprised at my new persona.

Few students were present in my homeroom when the teacher entered, pausing near her desk. "Goodness, Peter," the teacher exclaimed softly. "You're back."

I looked up and smiled self-consciously. "Good morning," I mumbled.

"You look well this morning," she added. "I heard." She sat at her desk then looked up. "If you'll stop by during your study period, I'll fill you in on missed lessons."

Gene entered, stopped at the front of the room, stared at me in feigned amazement, then faced the teacher. "Do you know when Pete's coming back?" he asked with a straight face, his lips quivering toward humor.

"Take your seat or leave the room until class time, Eugene," the teacher said.

Gene approached, sat at the desk across from me, his feet in the aisle, elbows on his knees.

"How're ya doing?" he whispered, "I heard you beat the shit out of John."

"Very funny," I said, but I couldn't help grinning. "How the heck did you know?"

"Some guy called Miller came around asking questions about you and Schauls."

The room began filling.

Gene stood and said, "Better get to my seat. See you at noon or study hall."

The morning went well, but during chemistry class, Bud Lange paused in front of me. His face was ruddy with loathing, his fists clenched. "Dirty Injun," he whispered through his tight lips. He continued on to his seat, leaving behind the odor of tobacco.

The rest of the morning was spent halfheartedly fending curious looks and pleasant smiles. In study hall, Gene sat down next to me.

"What'd your dad tell Miller?" I asked.

"You mean, what did I tell him," Gene said.

"Okay, then, what did you tell him?"

"Remember when we threshed at your place? Well, I told Miller how John bitched and punched you in the back when you was both behind the barn."

"How'd you know that?" I asked.

"I was taking a leak around the corner of the barn," Gene said.

"What'd Miller say?"

"Not much," Gene said. "Just that he was finding a place for you. How is it where you're at now?"

"I'm moving to a different farm, Miller says. Don't know where, yet."

Heading toward my homeroom after study hall, I met Mr. Zuelke in the hall. It wasn't always obvious, but casual meetings of students with Mr. Zuelke were almost always orchestrated.

"Well, if it isn't Mr. Razor," Mr. Zuelke said. "Well, well. New clothes, I see, and you look rested. How does it feel to be clean and well-dressed?" Then, as though to casually listen, he looked past my shoulder down the hall.

"Feels real good," I said.

Mr. Zuelke turned serious. "I talked with Mr. Miller. He tells me you were lucky."

"Maybe," I said.

"You really were, though unlucky to be with that . . . that character in the first place. Perhaps you can go out for football and other sports now. If it's all right with you we can work something out."

"I'm not big enough for football, am I?" I asked. "Not heavy enough, I mean."

"When you have a school our size, every sturdy boy is big enough. How much do you weigh now?"

"Dr. Steins said I was five-ten, 135 pounds or so."

"Yes, that's what he said," Mr. Zuelke agreed. "He said you should weigh 150." He chuckled. "Something tells me you'll start gaining weight right soon. Miller will find a good place for you." I smiled almost to myself.

Two, perhaps three days later, in gym class, Mr. Zuelke was called out and returned with a rare bright smile. Beckoning, he led me into the hall, where Mr. Miller waited.

"Good morning, Peter," Mr. Miller said. "Sorry about interrupting your class."

"Must get back to the class," Mr. Zuelke said. He smiled at me with a knowing look. "Hope you like your new home." He nodded at Mr. Miller and left.

"We've found a place for you, but you don't have to go," Mr. Miller continued. "After what you've been through, no one can blame you if you refuse, but you will need a home for at least two more years, and a farm is the best we can do." We started down the hall.

"If I can pull my weight, it should be all right," I said staring at the floor ahead as we walked toward the exit. "Did you tell them that I'm . . . I'm an Indian?" I hated meeting people for the first time—the twitch of surprise, the stuttered nonsense as they tried to talk off their astonishment.

"I don't think it was all that necessary with this family, but, yes, I mentioned it."

"John doesn't know where I went, does he? Did he call or anything?" I asked as I opened the door for Mr. Miller.

"I wanted to keep this quiet until we checked everything

out," Mr. Miller said as he passed me going through the doorway. He stopped just outside the building and reached to put his hand on my shoulder. I flinched, stepping back, and Mr. Miller withdrew his hand. "We contacted State Social Services couple of days ago, and John had not mentioned your leaving them. Nor had he called the sheriff or my office. My secretary called the Schaulses just yesterday, and it appears they had no intention of telling anyone of your disappearance. Also, in talking to your former neighbors, I learned John is mean to his wife, just like you said." We had walked to the car and he motioned to the passenger seat. "You're sure you want to try another farm?"

"If I can earn my way, sure. If you checked them out, they maybe aren't like John," I said.

"No, siree," Mr. Miller said. "Not this family. When I explained what happened, three farm families offered to take you. I know all three personally. Fine people. We selected a family expecting a child. They will need the most help. They're fair, you will miss no school for work, and will have days off. And, unlike at the Schaulses, you will be paid for summer work."

"Is anyone going to see Emma? I mean, to see if she needs help."

"Oh, that's right," Mr. Miller murmured. "Maybe I *should* mention it to the sheriff."

He sat in the driver's seat, looking out the windshield as he spoke. "We could go after John and Emma both, you know, for neglect, at least, but the law is funny about family things. The fact that you're seventeen, in good physical condition, according to Dr. Steins, makes it hard to nail John down. And John's relatives say he is a good man, that maybe you fell instead of being hit. They must know what he is, but he's flesh and blood, you see."

"He's got the shit scared out of Emma, too," I said angrily. Mr. Miller glanced sharply at me, but did not comment.

We turned onto the road to the Schaulses' farm. I stiffened. *He lied*, I thought. *He's taking me back.*

"I don't want to go back to Schaulses'," I blurted. "If he sees me . . . no telling what he'll do." My head pounded.

"We're only getting your things," Mr. Miller said calmly.

"All I have is old clothes," I insisted.

"That's it?"

"Well . . . a rosary and pocket Bible. Nothing else," I said. "I leave my books at school." My headache became excruciating as we approached and entered the Schaulses' driveway. Lowering my head, I avoided looking out the window.

"Stay in the car, let me handle this," Mr. Miller said, but I glanced up and was relieved to see that John's car was gone.

Mr. Miller talked through the screen door with Emma. Her anxiety seeped through the screening, and she seemed confused about what was happening. She disappeared into the house and returned moments later with a bundle of clothes and a pair of old work shoes. Cracking the screen door just enough, she handed them to Mr. Miller.

As we traveled south toward Caledonia, I could breathe easier, though I was still anxious about living with another family. A mile from town, we turned west.

"Mrs. Schauls couldn't find your rosary or pocket Bible," Mr. Miller said.

"That's all right. Didn't work for me," I muttered.

"How's that?" Mr. Miller said.

"Well, John prayed with the rosary . . ." I trailed off.

"Emma said John had trouble getting chores done the last few days," Mr. Miller said. "You were supposed to shred corn at the neighbor's." Smiling, he lit his pipe while steadying the wheel with one hand. "Serves him right."

"They're Gene's folks," I said.

Mr. Miller smiled calmly, "You're right, they're good people." He thoughtfully puffed his pipe, then said. "Say, Mrs. Schauls didn't give me your school clothes."

"Yeah, she did," I said, pointing my thumb at the back seat. "The ones on top."

"You went to school in those?"

As we approached a township road two miles west of town, Mr. Miller pointed through the windshield. "Your new home," he said. I stared at the farm a quarter mile away, studying it without blinking as we entered the farmyard. It was neatly arranged with a silo, dairy barn, hog barn, and a large, white house, surrounded on the north and west by a sheltering pine grove. Mr. Miller pulled up near the house, stepped out of the car, stretched, and walked around to my side. I rolled the window down.

"Come on, Peter, and meet the Klugs," he said.

Mr. Miller and I were halfway to the house when a young woman in her early twenties came out to meet us.

"Good morning, Leo," she said with a bright smile. "So this is Peter." She offered her hand. "I'm Pat Klug. Hope you like it here."

"How do you do," I said, shaking her hand.

Patricia Klug was mature for her age, brown hair, trim, and beautiful. Her pleasant manner threw me off balance.

"Come in," Pat said. Leading us, she motioned to the house, twisting to face me. "Lee, my husband, is out someplace. He'll be in shortly." Inside, Pat motioned to chairs, then to pastries on the table. "Have a seat, help yourself." She reached for a coffeepot and held it towards Mr. Miller. "Coffee?"

"Yes, thanks," Mr. Miller said. "No sweets, though." He patted his belly. Pat set a glass before me.

"Milk?" she asked.

"Yes, thanks."

The conversation was low, soft-spoken, intelligent, the likes of which were never heard in the Schaulses' house. I listened carefully, wary, but soon relaxed thinking back to when I last heard such talk—from Miss Crusely and Mrs. Cory. I didn't have a voice in my placement with the Schaulses, but now I had a choice, more important, the right, to choose where I lived.

Lee entered. He was tall, slender with brown hair and a mild manner. Lee and Pat had taken over the Klug family farm. One of Lee's brothers was a pharmacist in a city farther north, another was a part owner of the Caledonia Implement Company. Lee proudly spoke German, as did John Schauls, but Lee didn't seem to have the same prejudices.

"Well, Peter, I must get to chores. If you would, change clothes, meet me in the barn to see how we do things here." Lee talked quietly with an easy smile. I changed clothes and joined him in the barn.

"Well, here we are," Lee said. He smiled and motioned about the milking aisle, "The Klug milk factory." I smiled awkwardly and lowered my head to keep it private. A three-unit surge milker system was used for milking thirty milking short-horn cows, give or take, as some freshened or dried. We talked, both of us, during chores that first night.

The Klugs discussed things in a manner I had never heard at the State School or the Schaulses'—*How were things at the Schaulses'? How's your head and arm? We hope you like it here. Be sure to let us know if you have a question about anything.*

Still, I could not talk about the State School or my life at the Schaulses. The Klugs had been given sketchy information about why I left Schaulses'. And when the state approved my new placement, there was no reference to foul play. A note from the Klugs in my records requests more information from Miller about the Schaulses' treatment of me. There is no reply.

Early chores went quickly, and supper was a grand affair.

"Sure you've had enough?" Pat asked.

"Stuffed," I said.

As at the Schaulses', early chores meant feeding the cows and other stock, then preparing milking equipment. After supper, we milked from about six-thirty to after eight o'clock. After milking, we bedded the cows and made sure the young stock, hogs, and the hen house had water and feed. After we talked in the living room that evening, Pat took me upstairs to a beautiful bedroom with curtains, a polished floor, a dresser with mirror, and a cushioned chair.

I lay in bed that first night swimming in thought. It all seemed too good to be true. Images of my first months with John loomed in the darkness and his voice, his icy stare, haunted my sleep. Awakening, I sat straight up in bed and stared out the window.

12

My dreams were haunted by memories. Not only of the blow John had landed against me, but also the frozen image of him striking Emma, and the hammer Miss Monson swung from over her head. Each time I woke, I had to remind myself where I was. I was far now from the tiny attic room warmed only by a candle, far from the hospital ward where I listened to the train whistle, far from the cottage bed where I first heard the name locust, *and listened to the sound of its singing.*

. . .

At breakfast, the day after I arrived at the Klug farm, Pat seemed concerned.

"Did you sleep well, Peter?" she asked.

"Guess so."

"Just wondering," she said. "You screamed last night. Must have been a nightmare."

"Can't remember," I said.

"Just as well, the way it sounded," Lee added, smiling.

My first Saturday with them, Lee took me to repair fences. I fully expected him to leave me there and return to the house or go to town, but he worked with me until dinnertime. I was allowed to relax with them in the house, that afternoon, until chore time. We went to Mass Sunday and visited Pat's parents on another farm close by. Missing no school for work, I was allowed to participate in one sport and had every other Sunday off, including chores. Lee took the other Sunday off. Every day after school, Pat had a sandwich and glass of milk waiting for me. "Something to hold you over 'til supper," she always said.

In the two weeks after arriving at the Klugs, I began to feel better in a family setting, though still, on occasion, beset by sudden anxiety. Making friends with the neighbors, I discovered that three boys within a mile radius of the Klugs were from church or county orphanages, but none had abusive guardians. The Palen family had a number of boys, their own, two near my age, with whom I spent time during my Sunday off. Though it was exciting moving so fast into a normal world, I found it nearly overwhelming trying to adjust.

It was Friday, overcast and dreary my second week at Klugs. Lee was gone when I returned home from school, but he was often gone to town on farm business, and I wasn't concerned.

"When's Lee coming home?" I asked while eating my snack.

"It's chore time. Soon, I 'spect," Pat replied. "It drizzled on and off, today, and he's been in town all afternoon playing cards. Probably hanging one on."

"In the bar?" I asked.

"Yep. The guys get together like that on rainy days.

"I'll check the furnace," I said, becoming nervous, heading for the basement.

I sat on a fruit crate near the furnace mulling the approaching confrontation, which I was certain could only end with Lee beating me. A car slowed for the driveway, and I stood on the fruit crate watching as it passed the window. Stepping off the crate, I stood staring at the floor. I couldn't hold it and released urine just as the exterior door opened upstairs.

But I heard strange sounds upstairs—laughter, joking. Then the basement door opened and Pat, still laughing, called down, "Peter, you didn't finish your sandwich. Lee's home and he'll need your help doing chores tonight. Especially tonight!"

I climbed the stairs, still afraid. Lee smiled as I entered the kitchen, reached to put his arms around my shoulder, but I pulled away. He looked down and caught sight of my wet pants.

"Hey, no one's going to hurt you, Petie," Lee said, his smile still frozen while he cast a questioning look to Pat.

Another Friday, Lee let me off chores early so I could bathe and dress, and two Palen boys picked me up for an outing at the Avalon Ballroom in LaCrosse, Wisconsin, just across the Mississippi river. More students from Caledonia were at the Avalon, which seemed to be a hangout for teens who could drink near-beer in Wisconsin at age eighteen.

My friends drank beer and wine, but I drank sodas, until I was grabbed, held in a chair while a boy held wine to my mouth. At first, I struggled, then swallowed the sweet wine. I felt no different and let them cajole me into a second glass. After two more, the boys let me go, and I stood, immediately falling to hands and knees, then lay on my back staring up into smirking faces. One of the boys realized what they had done and I was helped outside where they walked with me around the building until I could walk unaided.

I learned more about alcohol that night and, the next morning, as Pat and Lee smiled, about hangovers. I understood at last that alcohol did not necessarily make people violent. As the weeks passed, I grew stronger and, as I came to terms with one new experience after another, I began to understand the workings of a normal world. Those new experiences gave me confidence in myself. I still tried to avoid trouble, but would no longer give way to bullies.

The windows of the chemistry classroom overlooked the athletic field. The field was crisscrossed, after a December thaw, with muddy walking trails and widely scattered patches of snow. It was the end of chemistry hour.

"I want your names on the upper right-hand corner of your work booklets," Mrs. Hefty said. "Bud, would you collect them, please?" As I hunched over to sign my booklet, it was violently jerked from me, and my pencil coursed a scraggly line across the cover.

"Have to collect yer booklet, Injun," Bud sneered, waving the booklet once in my face.

"Hey, what'cha doing, Lange!" I hissed, jerking upright and snatching it back. My back to the bully, I bent over my writing platform again, muttering almost to myself, "I have to write my name on it so's Hefty knows whose it is."

From side vision, I saw Gene and another boy frantically motion at something behind me, but I responded too slowly. Shoved hard in my back, I fell horizontally atop my own chair-desk, which tipped, carrying me into Gene and the other boy. We tumbled first into each other, then into the wall before sprawling on the floor. Gene was at the bottom of the pile. I was on top, only ruffled, and quickly rolled off as Bud aimed a kick at me.

"Son of a bitch," I shouted, ducking the kick.

"Bud Lange! That was uncalled for," Mrs. Hefty shouted. "I see it's time for you to visit Mr. Collins again."

Our principal was a fair woman and strict, but Bud sassed her terribly, it was said. When misbehaving, he was referred immediately to Mr. Collins, superintendent of schools, with an office in the high school building. He might have played college football, was tall enough to have played basketball, and he walked light-footed with long arm swings. Talking softly during disciplinary sessions, he had the full attention of those brought to his office.

As we filed out of the classroom, Bud sidled alongside and jostled me roughly into the door frame, hissing, "I'll see you behind the school at lunch hour, squirt, unless yer yaller!" At noon, I ignored the threat, going as usual to study hall where friends and I talked about Bud.

"He thinks no one will help you," Gene reminded me. "Especially since you left the Schaulses'. Take you being Indian and all, he thinks someone will give him a medal or something for putting you in the hospital."

"But you said he bullies other kids, too."

"He takes his points where he can. He thinks everyone hates Indians, which ain't true, and that others'll praise him for beating you. That kind of thing."

"I know, but I wish he'd pick on the football players," I muttered.

"He's not that stupid," Gene said. "He knows enough to protect his own skin."

"Suppose, I could carry a knife or something," I said scanning the study hall. A dozen boys and girls studied quietly and a teacher sat at the monitor's desk. I frowned as Bud suddenly appeared in the doorway glowing with anticipation.

"You ready?" Bud hissed. His manner said he wanted to do me proper. Others looked up and the study monitor seemed annoyed.

"You can't make me fight," I said, loud enough so the others could hear.

"Then yer yaller?" Bud yelled. By now, it seemed, everyone stared.

Glancing around at expectant faces, I closed my books and stood.

"I'm coming," I said half under my breath.

"He'll kill you," Gene said, tugging at my sweater sleeve.

"Maybe," I said and shrugged. "Would you fight him? You're stronger than me."

"Tell Klugs," Terry whispered across the table. "Maybe they'll talk to Bud's pa."

I took fifty cents from my pocket. "Could you watch my books and hold my money?"

"Okay, but I'm coming, too," Gene said.

I didn't know how to avoid such confrontations, so I just followed Bud, as I had followed Miss Monson or Mr. Beaty during punishment sessions. Others followed me, creating an unusual entourage making its way behind the school building. Swaggering in the lead, Bud was pumped with confidence, sure that the beating he was about to deliver would have admiring witnesses. It didn't matter to him that he was older, stouter and much heavier than me—that two of me could all but hide in his shadow.

I squared off to Bud and squinted aside at Gene, Terry, and other students I knew, then Kathy. Strangely, I assumed a State School slapping posture, arms by my side staring at Bud's shoulder.

"You can call this off any time you want!" Bud said. "If yer yaller!"

"I'm not calling it off," I replied without lifting my arms. Suddenly I was struck on the side of my face and knocked, stunned, to the ground. Propping on my elbows, I tried to understand what got me into that crazy mess in the first place. I had done nothing to Bud since arriving at Caledonia High except avoid him. Lying there a moment also gave me time to decide whether a fight with Bud was worth anything. He had a powerful jab and I wasn't eager for another. Glancing again at Kathy only yards away, I surged with disgust for allowing Bud to humiliate me. She leaned forward, a hand on her mouth and an "oh-my-God" look on her face. I wanted to change that look.

Bud stood over me—like Mr. Beaty in the garden—legs apart in a stance of victory. His sneer said it was easier than he hoped. I charged and swung, but was thrown down and kicked. Bud was just too heavy to manhandle. I would have to find a way around his bulk. He grabbed my sweater, tearing it to shreds as I twisted in his grasp. Grabbing his shirt, I kept much of it in my grasp as I was thrown to the ground. Bud kicked my ribs, nearly knocking the wind out of me. In a fluke, I bounced on my back, thrusting desperately upward with my legs. My shoe struck something hard that gave way with a crunch. Bud squealed in pain, reeling backward. My shoe had violently snapped his head back, splitting his lip and bloodying his nose. After further exchange of fists and shoes, during which he hung back more, I used my legs and feet more than fists. Bud suddenly became more cautious, and I had more time to plan and execute moves. Swiftly and accurately, l lashed out with my feet, hitting his shins, arms, and chest. All that walking to the school bus and hiking the bluffs at Rushford had done it. Bud feinted, backed off, feinted again, mostly for the benefit of onlookers. I stood, followed him until he feinted, then quickly fell backward, lashing a shoe square in his chest that sent him reeling back. If Bud's arms were stronger than mine, my legs were stronger than his, and with good extension.

Suddenly, a voice called from an office window, "You two! In my office, immediately!" It was Mr. Collins. The spectators scattered. Bud was bent, bleeding from his nose and spitting blood. I was flushed from fighting, my ribs were sore, my face had a bruise and my nose dripped slowly. I walked alongside Bud toward the school. Later, I would learn that Bud had lost at least one of his teeth.

"Yer lucky he stopped us," Bud wheezed.

I paused. "Wanta continue?" Though I was tiring, my confidence had been given another boost.

"We'd be expelled," Bud said. He didn't look at me, and his voice had lost its superior tone.

Mrs. Hefty came out as we entered Mr. Collins' office. Standing before Mr. Collins' desk, I was shirtless with a shred of sweater draped over my shoulder. Bud's shoulder-strap underwear was intact but covered with muddy shoe prints.

"The rules are clear. No fighting on school property!" Mr. Collins said. "If I hear of more fighting from either of you, I will have no choice but to expel you. Is that clear?" He looked from Bud to me, then back to Bud. I nodded agreement, though Bud looked out the window.

"Bud! Mrs. Hefty tells me you provoked the fight in chemistry class. Is that right?" Bud did not reply, but grunted something noncommittal.

Mr. Collins looked at me.

"Even if you didn't start it, you can't fight on school property. You have also violated rules. If Bud bothered you, you should have walked away or told someone."

He sighed, stood, and walked around the desk towering over us. Bud stepped back, but I had nothing to fear from Mr. Collins, so I stood my ground. "You can't attend school looking like that. You're both excused for the afternoon." Bud left immediately, and I waited in the office for Pat to pick me up.

I felt awkward the day after the fight and quietly read at my desk before opening bell.

A girl entered, approached my desk from behind and whispered in my ear, "Good going, Pete!" Her hand touched my shoulder as she passed. Then Kathy came in from her classroom just to say something. I blushed and was further embarrassed when boys entered, patted my shoulder, and said good things before moving on. It seemed everyone knew about the fight. There was little time between praises to relax, but I began to understand the depth of Bud's bullying. A State School boy, too naive to run from punishment or misery, had finally been pushed until he fought back.

Making my way down the hall after lunch, I saw Mr. Collins approach from the opposite direction. As when staff approached at the State School, I dropped to one knee and pretended to be tying my shoelaces, but he was heading for me anyway. The boys' room was nearby and, with attempted nonchalance, I stood and entered going to the urinals along the far wall. The door opened, long strides approached, and a large man stood at the urinal next to me.

"You're a hard boy to catch, Peter," Mr. Collins said. We both stared straight ahead.

"Oh?"

"I wanted to tell you privately, not that I condone fighting, that you did a wonderful thing for the school, and for Bud, too, perhaps. Hopefully he'll stop to think now when he bullies smaller boys." After Mr. Collins left, even after the door closed, I stood wondering why my fight with Bud had brought so much positive attention to me.

Months after the fight, I arrived home from school to find Pat unusually solemn. "Bad news," Pat said, handing me a sandwich and pointing to a glass of milk on the table. "Mrs. Schauls died. The funeral is tomorrow."

"He killed her, didn't he?" I said.

"Natural causes, they say. Internal bleeding," Pat said.

"How can internal bleeding be natural?" I asked. "Would I have died from natural causes? Bleeding in my head?"

Pat tried to calm me. "Every situation is different," she said. "We don't know the circumstances. Do you want to go to the funeral?"

"Do you think I should?" I asked, unsure whether it was proper.

"If you don't go, it might not be wrong, but if you go, it could never be wrong."

"It would be best to go, I guess," I said. "John wouldn't try anything. Would he?"

"Lee and I talked about that. We don't think so, but Lee would go with you just in case. And you wouldn't be waiting around afterward to be picked up."

Lee took me to the funeral and we sat in the back of the virtually empty church. John's and Emma's relatives occupied the first pew on both sides of the center aisle.

I had not seen John since leaving him, and I wouldn't walk past the open casket now. I felt sorry for Emma, but I could hardly pay attention to the service. I kept thinking that this was no accident. Staring at the back of John's neck, I heard little of the sermon, sure that any moment he would turn around and glare down the bridge of his nose at me. But he never did. Lee and I shuffled out as the service ended. It was the last time I saw John.

EPILOGUE

After the funeral, Emma's family took her body back to East-
man, Wisconsin, for burial. She had just turned thirty-nine
years old. It wasn't until years later that I found out her official
cause of death was complications from childbirth. It came as a
total surprise to me, since I hadn't even known she was preg-
nant. John was left with the two-week-old baby girl, as well as
the other three children, now six, three, and two, but he did not
shoulder that burden alone for long. On September 2, little
more than seven months after Emma's funeral, John married a
widow with three sons and a daughter. They moved to Hokah,

just a few miles northeast of Caledonia, but, as easy as that, any memory of what John had done was wiped away. He had a new farm, a new family, and no one knew who, or what, he was.

It was harder for me, and had I not met the Klugs, my view of life would have been much worse. I suffered recurring bouts of anxiety and depression, the first before the age of nineteen. I was on my own by then but still legally a ward of the state, so I was sent to the university hospital in the Twin Cities, where the doctors recorded:

Peter is hyper-anxious and makes himself physically ill. This is confusing considering that his entire childhood at the State Public School was such a stable and well-regulated environment.

Not long after, I was drafted into the army, a different kind of regimen than the State School. I rejected an offer to attend Officer Candidate School and an appointment to counter-intelligence school. Before I knew anything tangible about the electrical industry, at the age of 21, I was made the electrical supervisor of twenty Korean electricians and five GIs. I received three bronze stars—though I'm not sure what they were for—before rotating back to the States one month after an armistice stopped the fighting.

I learned basic electrical theory and practice in Korea, and, as a civilian, I studied electricity on my own. I became an electronic technician, journeyman electrician, and hobbied in HAM radio for decades. Along the way, I raised three children, Tom, the oldest, Kathy, and Janice the youngest. All three are married and have given me six grandchildren.

The prejudice I encountered all my life compelled me to

investigate my heritage, to discover why it seemed so terrible to so many. I studied Indian culture, my roots and, contrary to what I heard as a child, found it beautiful. I learned from reading Frances Densmore's *Chippewa Customs* that my great-grandmother, Mrs. Frank Razer of the White Earth Reservation, was well known for her beadwork.

When reading could take me no further, I began talking to tribal elders, learning about traditional customs directly from them. I enrolled as a member of the Fond du Lac Band of Ojibwa, where I learned to dance and participated regularly in powwows. With the guidance of elders and extensive reading, I learned to make traditional garments and musical instruments—from deer-toe jingles and turtle-shell rattles to large drums built from hollowed-out cottonwood stumps.

I felt I finally was reconnecting with my roots, until, one day, my daughter Kathy asked me about trying to find relatives on the reservation. She had graduated from the University of Wisconsin—Eau Claire by then, but she had never met my parents and seldom heard them discussed. The explanation involved my abandonment, the State School, those awful days on the farm. It was hard for me to resurrect those old memories.

Over the years, Kathy occasionally asked about the State School and we talked. I made a list of memories and worked them into a rough sequence. One long day we made call after call trying to find my long-lost friend from my State School days, Dale Cole. We first found Don Cole, Dale's older brother who still practices law in Montana. Don was fifteen when the family broke up and went straight into farm placement. He directed us to Layton, Utah, where Dale and Faye Cole live. Dale and I renewed a friendship severed nearly fifty years before. Now, the Coles and I spend every winter together in the same town in Arizona and talk often throughout the year.

Janice called State Child Services in St. Paul to see about my childhood records and went with me to get them. Kathy and her husband, Jim Gilles, a schoolteacher who has a deep interest in literature, encouraged me to keep writing and were dependable sounding boards, offering advice as I progressed. I had most of the facts, but I wanted my children and grandchildren to understand what it was like for me then as well—how I talked, what I was thinking. I added dialogue and tried to bring each scene to life, as though I were reliving that childhood.

The State School was closed in 1945. Today only a few of the cottages remain, and the Main Building has been transformed into the Owatonna State School Museum. When I went there to visit, I found among their collections an old 16-millimeter film shot there in 1930s. I sent a copy to Dale and got one for myself. I didn't expect much from it, but I thought we could at least have some shared relic of our childhoods.

When I watched the video, however, I saw one little boy who looked different from the others in the nursery. The mannerisms were familiar, and the face of that little boy looked like my daughters when they were young. To be certain, I asked my daughter Janice to watch the film. I didn't tell her of my suspicions; I just watched. When that boy came on the screen, she began to cry, and I knew for sure it was me. That grainy film of myself and one group shot of all the boys at the State School, taken in 1938, are the only childhood pictures I have.

Other than the Main Building and the scattered remaining cottages, the only physical reminder of the early days of the State School is the child cemetery. Nearly two hundred children lie there; some have headstones, but most have only a wooden cross bearing a name. In 1994 the Lutheran Brotherhood placed a guardian angel at the corner of the cemetery to keep watch over the children. I consider myself lucky not to be among those buried there. I finished out my adolescence with the Klugs, who showed me a different life. I went fishing, hunting, swimming, and learned at last what it meant to be boy, without fear of abuse. When I turned eighteen, I went out on my own, into the world.

One of the first things I did with my newfound freedom was to seek out my brother Arnold. I have a photograph of the two of us together taken near Bruce Crossing in Michigan's Upper Peninsula. It was a clear, early winter day, so we posed outside in front of the barn on the farm where he was working. We each have one arm wrapped around the other's shoulder, but my head is tilted away and there is a wide space be-

tween us. And it would only widen. He was already drinking, and it was impossible to establish a real relationship with him. Soon I returned to the Twin Cities to look for work. What I see most when I look at that photo now is the hard years ahead, the difficulty I would encounter trying to find out who I was and where I came from. My children have been my joy, and they have saved me. Seeing them grow into happy, healthy adults has helped ease the pain of my childhood, but nothing can ever erase the memories.

I'm still haunted by those seventeen years.

While the Locust Slept was designed and set in type at the Minnesota Historical Society Press by Will Powers and printed by Maple-Vail Press. The typeface is Kepler, designed by Robert Slimbach.